ANNI:
A FATHER'S STORY

WITHDRAWN

ANNI:
A FATHER'S STORY

VINOD HINDOCHA
with
SHEKHAR BHATIA

Mirror Books

Published by Mirror Books,
an imprint of Trinity Mirror plc,
1 Canada Square,
London E14 5AP, England

www.mirrorbooks.com
twitter.com/themirrorbooks 🐦

Mirror Books Editor: Hanna Tavner
Design: Susan Topping and Paul Mason
Editor: David Morgan

ISBN 978-1-907324-58-1

364.1523

Printed and bound in Great Britain by CPI Group (UK) Ltd, Croydon, CR0 4YY

In loving memory of my beloved daughter Anni

The Hindocha family have asked that all the
proceeds due to the family from the sale of this
book be donated to a charity in Anni's name.

ACKNOWLEDGEMENTS

Firstly, a special thank you to Shekhar Bhatia for his assistance in helping me to write this book.

I would also like to thank my entire extended family for simply being there for us. Always.

To the Facebook group "Justice for Anni" – thank you. You have never stopped fighting for my beloved daughter.

Thank you also to Anni's friends who shared their stories for this book. I will always be grateful to you.

To all my friends who have supported my family and I throughout this time, thank you.

Lastly, thank you to the many people all over the world who never met Anni but have shown their support is so many wonderful ways. I thank you from the bottom of my heart.

Vinod Hindocha

CONTENTS

Chapter 1

They have taken Anni

Mariestad, Sweden
Saturday, November 13, 2010

The phone woke me just after midnight. I'd been in a deep, peaceful sleep, not unusual for me back then but I was probably more tired than usual because a weekly volleyball match earlier that evening had taken a lot out of me. The guys are very competitive and always play to win and, frankly, though I wouldn't normally like to admit it, I'm not as young as I used to be.

It took me a few seconds to wake properly and realise the phone was ringing. I answered and heard the newly familiar voice of Prakash, the father-in-law of my recently married daughter Anni.

"Vinod, Anni and Shrien have been kidnapped. They have released Shrien but Anni is with the kidnappers. They have taken Anni."

Anni. My beautiful youngest daughter Anni. I had only just seen her get married to her new husband, Shrien. Anni, who at that very moment was – or so I'd thought – enjoying her honeymoon in South Africa and the start of their married lives together.

Somehow I was able to compose myself and ask Prakash what had happened, what was known. I tried to keep my voice down so as not to wake my wife Nilam. I failed. Nilam must have sensed something was wrong. She hadn't heard the full conversation but that didn't matter. It was the middle of the night and Nilam had overheard Anni's name. She knew it was terrible news being given to me. She looked at me and, through her tears, simply said: "Anni is never coming back."

Prakash told me the couple had been kidnapped on a highway in Cape Town but there was no news of Anni's whereabouts or who the kidnappers were. "We are trying our best to find out more," he said.

"What do they want? Do they want money?" I asked. Surely we could sort this? If these people had demanded a ransom, surely we could pay them off to get Anni back?

"Have they put any price on her? We'll go there now and pay whatever they ask," I repeated.

Prakash replied: "I don't know much but I'll keep you informed if I hear anything."

We needed to get to South Africa as soon as we could, and agreed to look for flights immediately.

After Prakash hung up, I called my brother Ashok and told him what had happened.

"You have to come here now. Something very bad has happened. Please come now," I asked him.

I was now wide awake. Sitting in the living room Nilam, our son Anish and I just stared at each other. None of us really knew what to say. Nobody really understood what had happened. I put my head in my hands, I just couldn't believe what I had heard.

The crystal lamp was lit and I caught sight of a photo of Anni posing as a model on the window shelf. She wore a blue dress, her face had been made up beautifully. She must have been around 15 in that photo. My precious daughter Anni. She looked so innocent.

Anish called his sister Ami in Stockholm and told her. We hadn't wanted to – we didn't want her to know anything until we knew more. She would only worry, but Anish insisted that she had the right to know. Understandably, Ami got angry and upset. She had a lot of questions which were impossible for me to answer. I did not have any more information. "Why did they even go to South Africa?" she cried. Like her mother she said: "Anni is never coming back."

Nilam continued to cry. I tried to reassure her: "Look, she's not dead... Please don't cry."

But Nilam was worried. Frightening thoughts were running through her mind. What if Anni had been raped? What if they were hurting her? She kept repeating: "What if she never comes back?" It was a devastating scene. I wished this nightmare would end.

Only a few minutes had passed since the phone call and yet our life had already changed forever. I'd heard the words every father must dread – one of my children was in danger. Now my wife was screaming and my son was walking around and around in anguish.

I would give my life for my children and this was one of those moments I had dreaded all my life, but never felt would come true. How could it? We were the Hindocha family. We had never done any wrong to anyone and were peaceful, giving and loving. My children had always been safe.

Besides, my daughter was on honeymoon. FOR GOD'S
SAKE. Her honeymoon. It was the beginning of a new life
with her husband. Why? Why? Why? Where was God when I
needed him now?

I felt like collapsing. My legs were giving way and my head
was spinning. But I knew that there was work to be done to get
Anni back and I needed to be strong. Anni needed my help.

I was about to go online to check the flights when Shrien,
my son-in-law, called. He seemed breathless and was sobbing.
I begged him for some news. Shrien replied, "Sorry, Dad. I
could not take care of your daughter."

On hearing these words, I straight away said: "Why are you
saying these words? She's not dead yet, is she? We'll pay them
whatever they ask and we will get her back."

Shrien didn't give me many more details. He just kept
crying, not making any sense.

I told him his father and I would be there as soon as we
could and we would pay the kidnappers whatever they
wanted. There was no way that my daughter would come to
any harm over money.

Shrien kept repeating the same words to me: "Sorry, Dad. I
could not take care of Anni."

I tried to reassure him: "Please, Shrien, don't cry and don't
worry. Everything will be fine."

By now Ashok had arrived. I could always count on him
to be by my side when I needed him. He called a Swedish
consulate emergency number which is there to help
Scandinavian people who have problems while travelling
abroad. It was important to remain focused on what needed
to be done.

We started to search the internet for tickets to Cape Town while more of our family members arrived at the house. I have a wonderful family and it was comforting to see them. While they looked after Nilam I had to get on with finding the flight, booking the tickets, getting to Anni.

The general agreement among us all was that we shouldn't worry too much because the kidnappers would want money and we would simply pay it. Trying to think positively, I reasoned that if these people saw the money they would let her go. We were pretty confident of that. Why would they take her otherwise?

I finally found seats on the Sunday afternoon flight. But Prakash had done better and said there were two tickets from Amsterdam to Cape Town on Sunday morning. I told him to book them. I would fly from Gothenburg, he would fly from Bristol – we'd meet in Amsterdam and travel to our children together.

I'd grabbed my suitcase and Nilam packed some clothes for me, neither of us caring whether they were for winter or summer. I was ready to go.

By now it was 3am. My flight was at 6am. The journey is normally about two hours' drive from our home in Mariestad. It was winter, dark and gloomy, with ice covering the ground and snowdrifts stacked high on the roadside. A horrible night and hour to travel on the roads but I remember demanding: "Someone take me to the airport now." Anish and my niece Mishalli needed little persuasion. In a time of crisis everybody wants to contribute or do whatever they can to help.

As we were leaving, I told the members of the family who had gathered that I was going to bring Anni home. Nilam's eyes filled with tears. Everyone else nodded at me – no one knew what to say.

Ashok hugged me and said: "Pay whatever these bastards want. We will get Anni."

I hadn't really thought how much the ransom would be. I had my credit cards with me and could withdraw whatever was needed from my accounts. The sum didn't matter. Anni did.

Even if they asked huge amounts I could arrange it within ten minutes because I have relatives that would support me and I was confident that they would be able to help and I would be able to pay them back eventually. Whatever amount was demanded, I could arrange it in no time through my contacts.

Money was not going to be a problem. That didn't bother me at all. If I had to pay, that would be fine. If I had to sell the house, that would be fine. Half a million rand, one million rand, whatever it took. Anni's safety was at stake, and finance was the least of my worries. Whatever they asked, we would give them.

There were no hugs or anything like that when I left the house. I was very determined and I wanted to keep my mind focused on Anni and getting her back from those who had taken her.

But inside my heart was breaking. Thinking of Anni made me feel as if my brain was going to explode along with my heart. My poor little darling daughter, where were you? I prayed that she was alright and that nothing bad had happened to her. I had to keep moving because if I sat down for five minutes, I felt as if I would drown in all our tears.

I didn't trust anyone else to drive. I could not afford to waste
even a few seconds and I could not, by any account, miss that
flight and fail to make the connection from Amsterdam to
Cape Town. The only way I believed I could make it was to
take the wheel myself.

I didn't even wave goodbye to the family as I manoeuvred
the Mercedes from the car port, reversed onto the street and
negotiated the difficult ice patches that had formed on the
drive.

It was a ghostly night with no moon. It was cold outside and
very dark, typical for Mariestad in November. Anish was next
to me while Mishalli sat in the back of the car. They both sat
in silence. I suppose they didn't know what to say. This was
not the time for small talk and they must have sensed how
agitated I was.

My head was full of thoughts about Anni. Please God,
I prayed under my breath, please keep her safe. My mind
drifted to thoughts of how they were treating her, if she had
been bound and gagged. Had they locked her up? Had they
given her food and water? How would they speak to her? Was
she blindfolded and tied up? I was determined to offer myself
instantly as a replacement for her freedom.

I genuinely believed it was possible that this was a
professional kidnap gang and all they would require was
payment to release her.

Not being in any way a violent man, I hadn't had a fight
since the school playground, but right now my anger was
more than I could handle. How dare they touch my daughter!

Despite the icy conditions I put my foot down on to the
accelerator until it touched the floor of the car. The E20 road

from Mariestad to Gothenburg was empty because of the hour, except for a few lorries with their blazing headlights. They moved over onto the inside as I flashed them and overtook. I knew I was speeding and at several places the traffic cameras flashed, but all I could think of was getting that flight.

Bizarrely, I remember thinking about how I'd inform the authorities on my return of the emergency mission which made me drive so recklessly. Even if I had to pay a fine, it wouldn't bother me. Nothing would have prevented me from making the flight except the weather.

The icy road was treacherous, and when we were about 30kms from the airport I nearly killed us all. Hitting some ice, the car left the road and flipped on to two wheels, almost as if it was happening in slow motion. It went into a skid that seemed to go on forever, even though it must have been around 20 seconds. I struggled with the steering wheel to regain control and keep the car on four wheels. In Sweden when you take your driving test you have to pass an anti-skid test and I remembered, despite the circumstances, not to brake but to steer into the skid direction as I had been taught many moons ago.

I had chosen to escape the highway and take a forest route which I reckoned would cut some 23kms from the journey. The narrow road runs through some small mountains and a forest. It can be dangerous to drive during winter time. The signs said you shouldn't drive more than 70km but the speedometer was hitting 110. The highway was full of bends and my mind wasn't concentrating properly on the dark road as more and more snow fell. I struggled to keep the car on the road as twice more we skidded onto two wheels and nearly overturned. It flew through the air, wiggled and actually left the road. The shock of feeling the wheels shudder as we hit tree roots and stones shook me into realising I'd put us all in danger.

"Calm down, calm down!" Anish screamed at me to drive carefully. He was absolutely right, of course. Thankfully, I managed to right the car as Anish reassured me we were nearly at the airport.

The drive had scared us all and I had to think about their safety as well as mine. Only I could rescue Anni – it was my duty as a father and I couldn't fail – but we had to be safe. I slowed down, but only marginally.

We arrived at the airport with just an hour to spare before the 6am flight. I knew that normally you have to check in two hours before an international flight and cursed under my breath.

Anish told me: "Be careful, Papa," but I didn't stop to say goodbye. Grabbing my case I rushed from the car and ran, not stopping until I had reached the check-in desk. I had just enough time to clear immigration and security and board the plane before the flight left.

My head buzzed with thoughts of how I could rescue my daughter, pushing out everything else. Suddenly, I felt exhausted. Once I sat in my window seat I struggled to stay awake and started to doze. But every so often I would suddenly wake as the horror of what had happened hit me and I'd think: "My God where is Anni now?"

The flight from Gothenburg to Amsterdam was a nightmare. At that stage I didn't know anything about what was going on in South Africa. Nobody called me and I couldn't call anybody. All I knew was my daughter was missing. Kidnapped, they'd said. Questions spun around my head. Where was Anni now? How was she? Anni was a strong girl, but I couldn't stop myself from thinking about all the horrific scenarios that could have happened to her.

Of course, no one at check-in or on the plane knew what I was going through. All around me were couples, parents with babies, elderly passengers and business travellers and I couldn't get over how normal everything seemed. Meanwhile my world was falling apart. None of them had any idea of the terror that was engulfing me.

Two hours later we touched down in Amsterdam...

I had 90 minutes' wait between my flight landing and the one for Cape Town taking off. Waiting in the transit area, I tried to call home, anxious to speak to my family and find out if they'd had any news.

But in my hurry to leave I had picked up an old mobile, only used as a spare in the family. Furious with myself, I realised I'd forgotten the pin code and knew I had only three tries before the anti-theft locking system barred me from using it.

Frustrated, I tried three times but kept entering the wrong code. It locked and I started to panic. By now, I was desperate for news of Anni and whether there had been a ransom demand from the kidnappers. I wanted to have the cash ready so that as soon as I landed I could give them the money and get Anni back. There was still time before the Cape Town flight that could be used productively. I could arrange the money and have it ready for the moment I landed.

I found a pay phone and dialled my home number. Ashok

answered and I told him it was me. That's when I heard crying and wailing in the background.

Ashok simply said: "They shot Anni."

He told me they had found her body.

I began to cry. "No, it's not possible. It can't be possible. I am on my way to get her. I am bringing her home alive."

Then I began shouting: "How can she be dead? It's not possible. I am going to get her!"

But inside me I knew as I heard the crying in the background that it had to be true. I knew Anni was no more. She had gone.

It seems that Ami had called the family with the devastating news her sister was dead. She had been informed by Shrien's brother Preyen who was in contact with the Cape Town police. They had found her body in the back of the car. She had been shot.

Now I was going to bring my daughter home in a coffin. Not holding her hand and hugging her like I'd imagined. Part of me kept thinking the police might be wrong and Anni was still alive. But the other part of me, the part that knew about the high crime rate in South Africa, that part slowly started to realise it was true. She must have been murdered. But I could not understand why. There was no reason for kidnappers to kill her if all they wanted was money.

There were so many people around me, doing such normal things, going to work, travelling on holiday or to see their loved ones. Some ignored the distraught man sobbing into the phone, while others looked at me strangely as if I was crazy. But none of them had any idea what had just happened, what I'd just heard.

Somehow I made it to the departure gate. I don't really remember how. I fell into a seat, unable to stop myself crying like a child.

Suddenly, Prakash appeared beside me and simply said: "Our daughter is gone." His other son, Preyen, had rung him on his mobile a few minutes earlier.

A very kind lady who worked for the airline brought me a glass of water and tried to console me. But by now I was weeping like a baby. I just could not believe it. My Anni. My Anni.

I could see Prakash was crying too, clearly distressed. But it was my daughter that had gone. He'd only known Anni for a few months.

I did not even hear the call to board the airplane. Everybody had taken their seats by the time the ground staff asked us to board too. Finding my seat, I closed my eyes.

Nobody should have to experience anything like that journey from Amsterdam to Cape Town. Prakash had a drink, advising me to do the same to help me sleep, but I couldn't. He ate his meal and fell asleep but for the whole flight I sat there crying.

My entire body and my mind were locked in shock. It was difficult to breathe and I could not focus. My eyes were hurting and everything was blurred. All sounds were muffled. I could not talk or listen. Every part of me was in pain. Grieving for my beautiful daughter, I felt absolutely lost and had no idea how I would get through the rest of the flight.

This was the first time I'd been to South Africa and I was going there to bring my daughter's body back.

Chapter 2

Family life in Sweden

Skövde Hospital, Sweden
March 21, 1982

Anni Ninna Hindocha was born on March 21, 1982, at the stroke of 6.47pm, weighing 6lb 3oz. Those around us in the delivery unit at Skövde Hospital would have heard both Nilam's screams during labour as well as my squeals of delight as I witnessed my precious second child make her entry into the world.

It had been a difficult day for Nilam with the eight-hour labour being both tense and painful. I had held her hand throughout as the gas and air soothed the kind of physical pain I know I will never have to experience.

Because of the complications that Nilam endured during the birth, it was a whole week before mother and child were allowed home. My wife had lost so much blood she needed several transfusions and the best medical care to aid her recovery. I will remain ever thankful to Nilam for what she endured, as well as what she had given us – another healthy daughter. I could not believe how life had worked out.

I'd grown up in Uganda in a house with corrugated metal roofing. My father had left India in 1936, aged 18, because he wanted his future family to be free and to grow up in a beautiful country without any restrictions. Africa afforded him that.

We were naturally a cheerful and contented family. I grew up with two brothers and two sisters and we remain as close today as we were throughout childhood. My parents kept us all closely under their wings and I instinctively did the same with my own children.

When I went to university in Bangalore I would return to Uganda each summer and simply laze in the glorious sunshine, never failing to be amazed by the natural beauty of an African sunset. It was a lovely upbringing, one I hoped I would be able to emulate when I went on to have my own family.

But in August 1972 Idi Amin ordered the expulsion of 80,000 Asians who, like my father, had been the backbone of the fragile Ugandan economy.

I felt betrayed, insulted and intensely pained at the news. Overnight my family were reduced to paupers. They were allowed to take absolutely nothing out of the country as they joined the endless lines at Entebbe International Airport to escape Amin's tyranny.

Crackly broadcasts on shortwave radios were often the only way I could establish what was going on in my homeland. I often became tearful at reports of people being slaughtered by Amin's henchmen and of others disappearing with his troops and never being seen again.

I felt so guilty that I was safe in India while my family lived in fear of the racist and power-crazed dictator that Amin had become.

After months of worry, word reached me that my family had been flown to Austria and were in a refugee camp with 4,000 other Ugandan victims. What a terrible flight to freedom it must have been.

Frustratingly, due to the circumstances, my contact with my family was minimal. A few months later they surfaced in Sweden and arranged for me to join them.

As I boarded the Air India jet to Stockholm I realised life in Africa as I'd known it was going to be a distant memory, a chapter I would have to put behind me and banish from my life forever. I cried many tears for the Africa that had been lost to me. My childhood dreams had been left behind and there was absolutely no hope of ever going back.

Little did I know that I would indeed be going back, but under the most horrendous circumstances some 38 years later.

Back then, the Swedes had given my family a chance to start again. When I eventually reached the town of Mariestad for that very first time, a three-hour train journey south of the Swedish capital, I was finally reunited with my family. I could have drowned in their tears. It was such a relief, such a joy to be in their loving arms again.

Our new home was a small town in the centre of Sweden next to Lake Vänern, the biggest lake in the country. It's a beautiful place with an old town filled with small, cosy houses and an impressive church tower that can be seen for miles. Tourists visit in the summer due to the beautiful lake and the nearby beaches.

My father and mother had found work picking strawberries and worked day and night. But despite social security being on offer, it was not enough to feed us all and to put my two

youngest siblings through school. I joined them picking fruit
and was paid around 4 kr an hour, about 33p, which I topped
up by working in one of the local factories.

All this came to a sad end when I was involved in an
accident in the factory, which resulted in my losing the middle
finger of my right hand.

The whole family had set about learning Swedish. Not only
had this been part of the deal in being invited to the country
but we wanted to fit in. Settle. People say learning Dutch is
tricky. I can honestly say Swedish is no walkover and although
we as a family are all fluent now, it took considerable time in
the classroom for all of us.

Soon after, I got a job at a local school teaching Gujarati to
displaced children from Uganda as well as maths and science.
After three years my father put his hand on my shoulder and
advised me it was time to find a bride.

It did not take long to find her. Nilam and I met through
family connections in 1976. They'd introduced me to this
beautiful young woman from Neasden in North West
London. Nilam was 25 at the time, a few years younger than
me. I was inherently shy but she made me feel relaxed by
chatting so warmly and openly.

Fortunately she was happy to move to Sweden, which
pleased me no end as I did not want to be separated from my
family again. After all, I'd learnt the hard way that home is not
a geographical place – it's where your loved ones are together.

Three months later we were married at Willesden Green in
England. Today my love for Nilam is as strong as it was when
I first set eyes on her. Maybe I love her even more now, if that
is at all possible. She is my equal and without her my life

would be empty. We have been through so much together, both good times and bad, but we've stayed really strong together.

When Anni arrived, our second beautiful daughter, I was overwhelmed with love and a sense of satisfaction. I appreciated the comments of relatives who were quick to point out that in our religion the girls were revered. Hindu goddess Lakshmi was the bringer of both material and spiritual prosperity, thus all women were regarded as an embodiment of beauty.

From the start, Anni was a bundle of joy, a beautiful baby with her dark brown eyes. As I held her I believed she was returning the beaming smile on my face. She had these lovely little hands and she was so small. It was like holding a piece of glass. Her skin was so soft and when she fell asleep in my arms, I had the most satisfying feeling inside of me. My little princess. She always looked so innocent and so peaceful.

At first we didn't know what to name her, Anni or Ninna. In the end we decided to keep both names, Anni Ninna Hindocha. I was at peace with the world. The elation of having two enchanting daughters, a loving wife and my entire family of parents, sisters, and brothers with me, was immense.

I still had to work as an electronics engineer for a local company but every spare hour I had I spent it with my little girls.

Ami took to her new baby sister extremely well. She loved her, although the newest child was a lot more mischievous and harder work than her elder sibling!

Anni hated bathtimes and she would scream the house down and the noise would be as terrible as it was funny. She also would not eat and even as a toddler, Anni fussed over the clothes her mother dressed her in, frequently throwing tantrums while trying to throw off the clothes she despised. It was an absolute nightmare trying to get her ready for nursery or to take her to the park. But these were individual attributes that I later came to admire in Anni.

As a baby she yearned to be near either her mother or me at night and we were half-aware when she would sneak into our bed in the middle of the night and snuggle up. Her trademark was to suck her thumb as she slept, while holding on to my ear with her other hand. Sometimes my ear ached as she held tightly onto the lobe. But we never pushed her away.

I suppose it was comforting for her to know her parents were near to protect her. I wish that had always been the case.

We had moved into a more spacious house around the time Anni was born. Before this, the entire family had shared a large house a few miles from the centre of Mariestad. But the addition of other family members' children meant we had outgrown the home and we all agreed it was time to live under separate roofs. This did not affect in any way the love between us all and, to this day, we are all extremely close.

The new house, a big white building, was located near the town centre. The upper floor had two apartments that could be rented out so we lived in the bottom floor and the basement. Over the years we have rebuilt the house to fit our needs.

In 1983, when Anni was one year old, my eldest brother Jayanti and his wife Sumi were also blessed with a daughter Sneha. She and Anni quickly became close friends. They went to different nursery schools but met almost every day. It was the perfect friendship and over the years the two became inseparable. They had no secrets from each other and were always there for one another.

I remember how we once hired a cottage some 120kms from Mariestad at Jönköping to visit a games festival. Anni would have been around six years old or so. All of us travelled in a convoy of vehicles from the cottage to the festival which was about 20 minutes away. When we arrived at the festival, somebody asked where the two cousins were. We realised they had been left behind like a scene from the classic film Home Alone. I drove back at breakneck speed worried that they'd be upset or frightened, only to find the two girls playing with their Barbie dolls completely oblivious to our terror. They hadn't even noticed that we were gone.

Those girls loved their Barbie dolls. My brother Ashok owned a number of gift shops and general shops in Mariestad and with his wife Nisha, as well as Nilam, they ran them with the help of support staff. Ashok would pick up Barbie dolls for the girls from sales reps. Once he even managed to obtain a pink Barbie car which Anni took great delight in pedalling around the garden during the summer months.

Anni was always perched on my lap or her mother's and when she wasn't she would sit in front of the television watching the cartoon Winnie The Pooh, being especially fond of the character Christopher Robin. She was very good at drawing from an early age and loved her art. But it was her Barbie dolls, along with Sneha, who were her best friends.

On countless occasions my mother, Ba, who is now in her 90s, told how Anni would lock herself in a room. All Ba could hear was my daughter talking to her Barbie and Ken dolls as if they were real people. She would sometimes close a door gently behind her and emerge to say that the dolls were asleep. Such an innocent and lovely little girl she was.

On September 27, 1988, Nilam and I became the proud parents of a son, Anish. Both Ami and Anni loved their little brother straight away. As a family we were complete. I had three gorgeous children and a wonderful wife. Life was good.

Anni and Ami were very close and loving sisters despite the five year age gap. They shared a bedroom during their early years and I would hear them chatting away before falling to sleep. Anni also shared a special bond with Anish, who was six years younger, but the person that she confided in the most was Sneha.

I was delighted when Anni gained admission to the local Flitiga Lisan primary school, which Ami already attended. For a while, they were able to study at the same place.

Anni wrote a book at school in Swedish, entitled: Book about myself. It had some very sweet hopes and dreams for her life, including meeting her Prince Charming, which she revealed in her own writing. It is something that Nilam and I will always treasure. It had her own illustrations, a picture of Nilam and two of her grandparents.

It read:

"For my future, I want to live in Mariestad, live in a house. A really nice one. I am not sure what I want to become. Maybe something like doctor, pharmacist, dentist, advocate detective or teacher. Or open a small shop with a friend or a cousin.

"I would often go travelling to Hawaii, Cyprus, Greece or some other warm place.

"Then I want to get married to a nice man and have two children."

Mariestad was a very safe, loving and happy environment for all of our children to grow up in. It didn't matter any more about the appalling circumstances that saw us move there. It was about seeing our children playing on the swings or walking around Lake Vanern. Safe and happy.

The greatest danger any of our children ever faced here was the risk of falling and grazing their knees while playing in the park.

That was the case in Mariestad all the time my children were young and it's still very much the case today. Only around 16,000 people live here and there is hardly any crime. We were among the first Asian families in Mariestad and we have never suffered any racism, none at all. The people of Mariestad have welcomed us since the day we arrived and, although we look different, we are part and parcel of the community.

People respect us because we work hard and believe in education for our children. This was, and still remains, a place where people say hello to each other, carry your shopping or invite you into their homes and expect nothing back. A sleepy place this may be, but it also has incredible charm and warmth.

I do sometimes think that perhaps a harder upbringing might have helped Anni deal better with the harsh realities that we all face in later life, but I would not change her childhood in any way at all. It was a privilege to raise a family in such a place.

Chapter 3

Arriving in Cape Town

Cape Town, South Africa
Sunday, November 14, 2010

That flight from Amsterdam to South Africa seemed to take forever. I was still in disbelief that Anni had gone. In shock. Perhaps it was my mind, or my heart, playing tricks on me. Maybe I refused or did not want to believe it. Whatever it was, I was not prepared to accept that she had actually been shot dead.

The air stewardess gave me water several times and at one time she even held my hand. I vaguely recall Prakash telling her: "This gentleman has lost his daughter in South Africa."

I had spent those long hours going backwards and forwards in my mind, in complete and utter turmoil. I wondered what could have happened, putting myself through torture as I thought about her last few minutes alive. What had they done to her? Was she in pain? Did they abuse her? Sexually? Did she cry out for me?

I had read a lot. I was more than aware that such horrific crimes and incidents took place in the world. I knew that they sometimes involved rape and very vicious assaults. That girls are sometimes found in pieces in South Africa. Slaughtered.

All those stories went through my mind as I thought about what could have happened to Anni. I prayed that if she were indeed dead, and I had to start believing it, that her ending was quick and painless.

Then anger set in. Why the hell did they murder my baby? I would have given them every single penny I had. I would have offered myself as a replacement if they had freed her. My life for Anni's and all my money and property. Everything. Anything. It just didn't make sense. Why kill her?

Just like during my flight to Amsterdam, I could not get over how normal everything seemed around me. I gather that's quite a common emotion for people whose worlds are falling apart. That you expect everything and everyone to stop. So to witness such normality, such mundane normality, is too much.

I felt it as I looked at the other passengers watching films on the in-flight systems, eating their meals, chatting with each other. All unaware that the man sitting in the seat next to them was broken and in hell.

Naturally, I would not have wished my ill fortune on any of these good people. But the routine and mundanity of the flight appeared to be, in its own way, disrespectful of my grief. There was no way others could have known, or indeed cared, about my situation. Life was going on around me and there was nothing I could do except sit strapped in my seat, drinking water and crying.

It was night-time when we landed in Cape Town. Dark outside. As we headed down the steps there were passengers queuing in front of me, taking too long. I wanted to leap over their shoulders to reach my Anni.

Getting through immigration, collecting luggage and

passing through customs is always a lengthy process, but that night it seemed to take an eternity.

Staff from the Swedish and British consulates met us inside the terminal and drove us the 20 minute journey to the Cape Grace Hotel where, so they told me, Anni and Shrien had been staying.

My head was pressed against the window. I looked out of the car windows at Cape Town and hated it straight away. I hated the roads, the houses and even the innocent and poor people living in shacks we passed.

This was the first time I had visited South Africa. It had taken my Anni and I was filled with an anger and despair I had never experienced before. Hatred.

In stark contrast to the desolate shacks we'd driven past before the driver took us off the N2 highway, I couldn't help but notice that there was also a lot of money for some people in the city.

The Cape Grace Hotel was lit up when we arrived around midnight but I could not appreciate its opulence. I just noticed its lights reflecting on to the water and thought what an elegant place for my Anni to stay. I knew that, like most fashionable young women, she would have loved its stylish hairdresser, swimming pool and luxurious restaurant.

I suddenly felt overwhelmed by my need to know everything, every detail of her stay. I needed to know if she'd been happy...

As we walked in, Shrien was waiting there in reception with about six other families. Apparently, they were South African Indian families who had come to the hotel to support him.

I later learnt one of them was Heather Raghavjee, whose

husband had also been murdered in South Africa. She had travelled from King William's Town to Cape Town after news of Anni's kidnapping and murder had broken.

Heather's daughter-in-law Alvita Raghavjee, who lives in the Bristol area and knew the Dewani family, had asked her to go and help. Shrien had never previously met her. But, coincidentally, her husband Dr Pox Raghavjee had also been murdered by car-jackers in 2007 – killed by a single bullet. The case remained unsolved. Mrs Raghavjee had made the journey out of respect.

As soon as she saw me walk into the lobby she started crying. She immediately told me she felt very sad for me, adding that she was also remembering her husband because he had died in a similar way.

It was one of those bizarre coincidences that happen from time to time. Two tragedies both created by mindless gangsters with guns. Two losses that were bringing people together.

Shrien greeted us at the entrance and we instantly hugged each other. By now I was crying again. Two distraught people trying to sympathise with one another through their own grief. I had lost my daughter and he had lost his wife.

In the foyer there was also a Swedish journalist Toby Torbjörn Selander of Expressen newspaper who had come to write about Anni's murder. I heard him speaking Swedish, possibly directed at me. I don't really know. I didn't really care. I was not in a state of mind to be interviewed or to even listen to him.

By now I was exhausted. Drained. Twenty-four hours had passed after that initial call had woken me up. Twenty-four hours had passed since our world had fallen apart. I was overwhelmed, incapable of doing anything more. I was totally exhausted and felt like I had aged ten years in less than a day. I was out of my mind and crying the whole time. I was running on empty, and in such pain that I knew I had to rest immediately.

But it was a busy time for travel in South Africa and the hotel was fully booked. Staff managed to find just one room for me to share with Prakash.

The woman from the Pretoria Swedish consulate, Kristina Ahberg, had not left my side since meeting me at the airport. She was very supportive and it was helpful for me to be able to speak Swedish with someone. English is my third language after Gujarati and I probably wouldn't make much sense speaking it. I wasn't making much sense of anything anyway.

Kristina found a room to stay in a nearby hotel and assured me she was only around the corner if I needed her help during the night.

Prakash, who was to share a twin room with me, told me: "Vinod, you go to sleep and I'll go and check on my son."

He didn't come back for the whole night, just left his luggage. He must have stayed in Shrien's room. I would have liked to have been there with him to listen to what Shrien told him, my need for information was so pressing. But my body gave into exhaustion and I finally slept.

The next morning I woke around 7am. Prakash came back shortly afterwards. I dressed and we went downstairs for breakfast. Shrien joined us around 8am. Kristina was already there in the lobby and I could see she was upset that I was still crying. But I could not stop.

I spoke to Shrien before we went in for breakfast. He was holding up remarkably well. Prakash and I listened as he told how he and Anni were kidnapped. They had been driving back from a restaurant when it happened. He said their taxi had been stopped at gunpoint by robbers and the driver was ordered out. Shrien said he was later thrown out of the car through the window and they took Anni away. He had flagged down a passing car and the driver called the police. When he made it back to the Cape Grace he was told that Anni had been shot.

I was struck by his strength. He was being so strong while I was being so weak. He was holding it together while I was falling apart. But then I had known Anni for 28 years – he had known her for less than two.

I don't know how I felt hearing Shrien speak. It's so hard to describe listening to the details of your daughter's death but I needed to know them. Shrien had told us some details but the story was still so incomplete.

I still had so many questions but the police said it was early in the investigation and they would keep me informed when they could. I had to try to be patient. I'd have the answers to all my questions and the details would come.

Once again it seemed the whole world was going about its normal, regular business at breakfast time. People deciding what to drink, what to eat. Again, mundane decisions, mundane tasks.

I couldn't eat, but forced myself to drink a coffee to keep me going. I was locked in hell. The knowledge that I would never see Anni again haunted me. She was no longer on this earth and that morning brought the reality home even more.

Prakash and Shrien ordered omelettes but I had no appetite. I was just thinking of my daughter. Kristina was sitting with us. There was zero conversation between me and Shrien and his father. I had no energy to talk and just wanted to be alone with my own grief.

Father and son were talking all the time but I didn't take in what they were saying to each other. If I felt excluded it was because my loss was far greater than anybody else's in that room. I wasn't myself. I had lost my mind. I was numb to everything and everybody. In my fog I remember there was another journalist on a separate table who came and asked for Shrien but Shrien sent him away.

All I wanted was to see Anni. I waited in the hotel lounge and at around 10am the police Captain Vinesh Lutchman arrived. Shrien told me the officer had helped him a lot and was involved in the investigation. I thanked him and as I looked at the officer I saw that he was of Indian origin like myself which, strangely, was a comfort to me.

He would understand how much daughters were cherished by good Hindu families and the mourning customs of my religion.

But right now that was irrelevant. I just wanted to see my daughter. Nothing else mattered.

I suddenly vented my frustration on my son-in-law. "I want to go and see Anni now," I said to Shrien. I just wanted to see her. I needed to see her.

But Shrien said no. "You can't see her today. She is totally drained out. She had no blood in her body. They have to put in liquid to fill her up and make her look good."

I was stunned. How could he utter such insensitive words

to me, a father who had just lost his daughter? Surely he understood my desperation. I didn't understand why he spoke like that about his own wife's body, and in public too. Besides, how did he know so much about the treatments carried out on a body once a person had died? I was angry now as well as sad. In fact, I was reeling.

Shrien was giving me very little comfort. Unlike me, he wasn't crying. He wasn't demanding to know what efforts were being made to find the shooters. He wasn't even hugging me. He just seemed more interested in his laptop and his mobile phone.

I stared at the floor as he sat opposite me typing away or making telephone calls.

I shook when I heard him raise his voice as he spoke into the telephone. He was having an argument with a relative back in the UK and shouted: "You don't interfere. I am going to do it."

It seems he wanted to organise something for when we returned to the UK but I didn't know what – only that it had something to do with a gathering to mark Anni's death.

After he had calmed down, he got back to his laptop. I knew the Dewanis had a very busy workload back in Bristol and assumed that maybe he was keeping his mind off things by concentrating on the family business. If it helped him, I was pleased, although there were no visible signs of him being upset. Perhaps it was just his way, to keep it bottled inside and busy his mind with normal things.

I left him to it. I just sat there with the officer hardly saying a word. I alternated between crying and staying in control. But mostly control.

Later that afternoon Captain Lutchman and I had a few moments alone. I asked him to tell me what had happened to Anni, what he knew. The officer patted me on the arm and said:

"Vinod, one thing I will tell you is that she wasn't raped."

It was such a relief to hear that there had been no sexual assault. Then it hit me there would be terrified family members back in Mariestad who needed to be told this. Especially Nilam.

I asked the officer whether he could do me a favour. I had brought a second mobile with me and put it into my suitcase on the plane in my haste to pack. I took it from my pocket and told him: "I am going to dial a number, then please can you say the same words to my wife?"

As he nodded, I was already dialling my home number and I spoke with Nilam, telling her there was a police officer with news. Lutchman took the phone from me and told my wife:

"Anni was not touched. She was not raped."

I could sense how relieved Nilam would be as she hung up and he passed the phone back to me. It was very important for us, Anni's family, to know her last moments had not involved a rape or sex attack. They hadn't defiled my daughter. I could see that the officer sensed my relief too.

It didn't take away the fact that Anni had been murdered, but at least her mother would find a little solace from that at this terrible time. I prayed for Nilam to have the strength to support Ami and Anish back in Sweden, and herself. She was recovering from cancer, and I prayed this would not affect her recovery. Although I could not be there for Nilam at this moment, I knew Ashok, Jayanti and their wives would be helping everyone.

I spent the rest of the day in the company of the Swedish consul. Shrien and Prakash had gone out. We walked from the hotel to the waterfront and had some food. My first meal in 48 hours.

That evening Prakash and Shrien returned and they had Captain Lutchman with them. I was sitting in the lounge reading the newspaper. The headline read: "Foreign Tourist Murdered." It started me crying again. But I learned more from the newspaper than Shrien, or anyone else, had told me. The report stated where they found Anni's body and what time she was killed. But it still wasn't enough information. I still didn't have any answers.

Shrien sat opposite me and went back to typing into his laptop and spending time on his phone. He took one particular phone call, got up leaving his computer on the table and disappeared into the lobby area, talking to his caller as he walked. He had an envelope in his hand and also a newspaper or a magazine when he rose from his seat.

He came back ten minutes later and sat at my side. I came to know later that this phone call was to be a key development in the investigation into Anni's death.

Chapter 4

Anni moves to the UK

China
February, 2010

Nilam and I were on holiday in China in February 2010 when Anni phoned us to say she was moving to the UK to stay with Sneha. She would be leaving for a new life in Luton on March 1.

The cousins were still very close and clearly missed each other a great deal. The pull of being together, reliving all the good times from their younger days and adding to them in Britain was too good to ignore.

Nilam and I discussed it at length. We both knew this was to be a major stage in Anni's life and, once she was settled in the UK, I doubted she would ever come back to live in Sweden.

I'm not too proud to admit that it was a difficult move for me to come to terms with. Despite the UK being a great country and London a fantastic city for all ages, it meant the final passing of the child into adulthood. I am sure I'm right in saying the majority of parents struggle with their children growing up and moving away.

Anni had already lived away from home. After sailing through her O and A levels at Vadsbo School in our home town Mariestad, she had gone to study at the University of Gävle, around five hours drive from us.

During her four years as a student she changed courses from electronic engineering to studying innovation engineering at the University of Halmstad. She moved because Sneha was already studying there and the distance between Gävle and Halmstad, around 700km, was too much. The two of them could not stand being so far away from each other.

As a father I would worry about my daughters being away from home, but took great comfort from the fact that Anni and Sneha had the opportunity to be together again.

In 2006, Nilam had been diagnosed with stomach cancer and had to undergo surgery. Anni, being the loving daughter that she always was, dropped everything, took a year off from her studies and moved back to Mariestad to help me care for her mother.

Anni helped no end and was always there for Nilam. She would give her the hope and strength that she needed to get through this tough time. I couldn't have been prouder of my daughter during this period in our lives. She gave up everything to be there for us and that is when I truly appreciated what a wonderful girl we had raised. During that year of being the angel of our dreams, Anni also developed a fantastic skill in preparing Indian food and her cooking soon became very popular in our household.

What an amazing young woman Anni was turning out to be. This was a girl so beautiful, both on the outside and the inside, and here she was, back in Mariestad, being the loving and supportive daughter. She had outgrown the town, but her heart remained at home with her mother. It was a hallmark of her generous nature.

I realised, though, that Anni wasn't coming back to live in Mariestad. She needed to follow her own dreams. I would be a fool to think that my daughter did not have a life of her own or a boyfriend or two. People all over the world have told me how beautiful she was. Still, there are some questions that a father shouldn't ask and I certainly didn't.

A year later Anni got a job at the electronics company Ericsson in Stockholm. She loved the freedom of the capital city and the opportunities it gave her. During the first year she stayed with Ami, and then with her cousin Neal, Sneha's brother.

Neal told me how Anni changed his way of living. Apparently she made his diet healthier and even got him into jogging around the two lakes near his home in Sundbyberg, north of Stockholm. I was pleased that once again Anni had the safety net of a cousin to keep her company but I knew that at the age of 22 she was fast becoming an independent woman.

When Neal informed me that a flat was for sale on the floor underneath his in the same apartment block, I jumped at the opportunity. I paid £50,000 as a deposit and told Anni to secure a mortgage on the remaining £120,000. She was earning well with Ericsson. I knew that if she didn't have a mortgage in her own name there was a risk that this young woman, with her fondness for clothing and buying presents for others, might fritter away her earnings.

Nilam and I so looked forward to the days Anni would come home to visit. I had made an agreement with her that we expected a visit every third week as part of the deal of helping buy her a flat and a car. She never broke her promise. And the days spent with her were just so beautiful. She would raise the brightness in our home with her smile and her passion for everything. All her cousins would descend on us and it was a sheer joy to have so many young people who clearly loved each other, and respected their elders, under the same roof.

On such visits Anni would love to sit in the sunshine. I built a wooden deck outside the house and Anni would sit out there for hours listening to music and enjoying the sun. It's a really warm spot as it's sheltered from the wind. Anni would put her bikini on and just chill out there looking out over the garden, the beautiful pink rose bushes and the little playhouse that has been out there since the children were small. Often her friends would come over and all of them would sit there on the deck, talking away. Just like girls do. Anni's friends were a very big part of her life. Whenever she was home, the house would always feel so lively and joyful.

Nilam would cook her favourite food and my brothers who live in the town would bring their children along so we were one big happy family. I would take a step back and look at everybody, listen to the laughter and the music, admire the charisma of the Hindocha clan and thank God at how lucky I was.

But now she was going abroad. Anni would have to be alone now, in a different country, away from the safe arms of her parents and she would likely meet somebody, fall in love and settle in the UK forever. I had always been the closest man to her but I knew another man would soon become her number one.

Sneha was equally excited to have Anni back with her and it

brought a smile to my face when I heard that Anni, who was unemployed after quitting her job in Sweden, would do the cooking and cleaning while Sneha went out to work with an electronics company to earn their keep. They were just like a couple. Inseparable.

We tried supporting Anni, although she found it difficult to accept money from her parents. I remember once forcing money on to her when she was leaving, only to find it stuffed behind the front door. She didn't want to take money from her parents. She wanted to be independent and felt bad taking our money. But Anni had a hard time keeping money. If she had money she would use it. So a few days later she rang and asked if we could put 100 kronor (£10) into her account as she had run out of money. I always gave her a little more than she asked for because I felt so sorry for her.

She tried hard to get a job in London in those first few months after moving there, including applying unsuccessfully for a job at Harrods and, later, in an office.

Still, Anni remained optimistic and made us all laugh when she told us she had bought a pair of high heels to wear to one of her interviews. She went wearing trainers because they would be easier to walk in. Her plan was to get to the bathrooms and change into her newly bought shoes there. But when Anni went to swap her shoes she discovered they were both for her left foot when she took them out of her bag. Well, she had no choice but to meet the interviewer with two left shoes on. How we laughed when she told us. These kind of things would only happen to Anni. Still, it didn't matter – she got through to the next round of interviews anyway.

Anni and Sneha had a tremendous time renewing their

friendship. If anybody was close to Anni it was Sneha and I am sure they knew all of each other's secrets.

Both were beautiful young women and would have been the centre of attention wherever they ventured into London. The toast of the town. When these young ladies dressed up, they dazzled. But these young women had a healthy self-respect as well as being respectful of their elders, proud of their backgrounds and emotionally attached to their families back in Sweden.

I have countless nephews and nieces in London and around the UK and they are all securely bonded and fond of each other. My sisters in Britain will think nothing of feeding a dozen young cousins should the occasion arise and it works that way throughout our family. We holiday together and sometimes my brother Ashok, who is the best at organising, will find himself having to book some 20 or 30 plane seats to accommodate everybody.

We work hard, extremely hard, but we also live life to the full and see each other as a family almost every day. Family is, and always has been, the most important thing.

Ashok and his wife Nisha have our respected mother Ba living with them. This was my late father's wish and it would have been the natural thing to do anyway as our respected mother is the head of the family.

My youngest brother runs the Mariestad Hotel in the centre of the town, assisted by Nisha and their daughter Mishalli. My elder brother Jayanti is up at the crack of dawn each weekday morning to help prepare the breakfasts for guests and is a master at producing the freshest salads for the lunch buffet which is very popular with locals. Jayanti's youngest daughter

Nira is the hotel's resident DJ and I put my background in electronics to good use by helping maintain lighting and wiring, and even the hotel's lifts. Jayanti's second daughter Nishma is a dentist and lives about an hour away, but is often seen around the hotel at weekends. Both my son Anish and Ashok's son Nikesh live and work away from home.

We take every opportunity to pull the family together whenever we can and one such family gathering was on November 27, 2009, when we were at my home to celebrate Nilam's 58th birthday.

Anni had brought home a young man called Shrien to introduce him to around 20 of the Hindocha clan. His name had been mentioned before as her boyfriend while Anni was in Stockholm. I had been intrigued but did not want to interfere.

A few weeks after she had left for Luton I was able to establish that that they were growing closer and he was one of the reasons why she left, because he lived in the UK.

As I've said, our family is very close and I soon learned that Nilam's sister-in-law had been the matchmaker. Indian families normally have an aunt somewhere among the ranks whose job it is to find suitable partners for the youngsters. They are both feared and revered but there is never any question at all of our youngsters being pushed into arranged marriages. They can arrange their own lives and are absolutely independent. Still, a little nudge in the right direction can sometimes be seen as a duty by the elders. This was the situation with Anni and this particular gentleman and, on the face of things, she had done her research.

She had established that this chap's family were called

Dewani and were from Bristol. She also found out that Shrien was approaching the age of 30 and still single. He was well educated and had a good income from the family business called PSP, which operated a number of care homes in the West Country.

Since the introduction and first few meetings he had been wooing my daughter by sending flowers to her desk and home in Stockholm from Bristol.

Anni was a romantic who told her cousins that one day her Prince Charming would walk into her life, and such romantic gestures would have appealed to her. She was being won over and enjoying the attention. I heard from family members that she liked this man. I was happy as I worried about her being alone in London when Sneha was working.

So I was delighted when Anni finally rang us a few weeks after leaving Sweden to tell us officially that she and Shrien had decided to go out together. She asked me: "Papa, are you OK with it?" I told her I absolutely was if she was happy but that it was her life. If I am honest, and I would be very sad if this was taken out of context, I was glad that he was a Hindu like us and had been well educated. What father doesn't want the best for his child?

Ami is happily married and they have two beautiful children together. We are all proud of them. My grandchildren. I love those kids so much. Ami and her husband Henning are good together and we adore her husband who is very close to us. We wanted that same happiness for Anni.

Shrien came to our house that day, November 27, and joined the 20 family members who had gathered to celebrate Nilam's birthday. That is why I remember the date so clearly.

We had been expecting him and the stakes were raised when Anni sent us a proposed timetable for their visit. She wanted us to make a good impression on him. Lunch, tea and a visit to the local Buffalo restaurant had been worked into the schedule.

But the day they arrived was something of a disaster. First of all Anni somehow got lost on a road from the airport that she had driven on countless times. The couple ended up being about one-and-a-half hours late. Secondly, all the food we cooked turned out to be inedible. The salad was watery, the aubergine curry tasted like petrol and we had no idea why. The lentil dal that Ba makes is usually delicious. But on this day, it was tasteless and even the rotis were too hard to eat.

When Ami's husband Henning and I went to collect Nilam's birthday cake, we dropped it on the drive outside the house and it landed upside down. Luckily it was in a box so I told Henning to say nothing and we might get away with it.

But when Nilam opened it and saw the mess of cream and strawberries, her face dropped. We didn't respond when she inquired what had happened. We tried to hide our faces.

Shrien made an immediate impression when he walked in and bowed to touch my wife's feet. Touching the feet of your elders is simply a mark of love and respect for them and a request for their blessings. Shrien had gained a gold star from the start.

He was handsome with a swathe of dark hair, a cheery smile and was soft spoken, almost to the point that I had to cup my ear to hear him speak. He shook my hand and then hugged me. I didn't mind him not touching my feet as we hadn't really brought up our three children to do it themselves.

But I realised that I was on show as well as Shrien. He was meeting me for the first time and, although it was my house, I knew deep inside that it would be wise to try to create a good impression and warm welcome.

After some tea and cakes, Anni surprised me when she suggested that Shrien and I spend some time together alone to talk. She whispered to me that I should "interview him."

He further surprised me when he addressed me as "Dad" when I drove around Mariestad, which can never take more than a few minutes. I pulled my Mercedes on to some land behind the golf course, stopped the ignition and asked him why he had called me that. It wasn't meant as a hostile response in any way but he appeared to be worried and said if he couldn't call me dad he'd have to call me uncle. I didn't want that, as nearly every Indian youngster addresses senior men close to the family as uncle. "Dad's fine," I said, realising then that something big was going to happen in Anni's life.

Shrien urged me to ask him anything I liked about his past. I said I was only interested in the future of my daughter. I told him I knew about his time at Manchester University, his successful health care company and how he had been introduced to my daughter. He was a stranger to me but he knew my daughter and she liked him. I wasn't sure how close they were, but she had brought him home and that was significant.

I also knew from other family members that he had been engaged once before but the relationship had floundered. I actually didn't care about his past. That was his life before he met Anni. After all, many young men of his age have had past relationships which have failed. I didn't want the details. There couldn't be anything he could surprise me with.

I felt he was a very nice guy, good looking, respectful and from a very well educated family.

"As long as you love her and take care of her and as long as Anni is happy, that is fine with me," I told him. He seemed a bit taken aback and repeated the question of whether I wanted to know about his past. It was almost as if he wanted me to delve into his background and help him reveal something which had been bothering him. I told him that everybody had a past and that we needed to look forward not backwards. I had no suspicions at all. Why would I? Neither did I have any expectations about him. As far as I knew, they had been dating a few months and that was that. I am not the interfering type and, yes, maybe I take people far too easily at face value. But Anni was happy. That is all that mattered.

That evening Anni and Shrien were invited to Jayanti's house and we played games while Anni did some impersonations of family members and was as usual the life of the party. The family spirit had been lifted by the fact that it was Nilam's birthday and Anni was on the arm of a handsome Gujarati man.

I recall Anni was trying to get close to Shrien by leaning into him and sitting cosily with him on the sofa. But he appeared distinctly unresponsive to her. I thought he was just being respectful to me. Nilam was more curious and asked Anni why she was clinging to him. Anni went quiet and stopped it. But the beer flowed. Things were looking good.

Later we returned home and Shrien stayed in a separate room. There was never any question of him sleeping with Anni that night.

Chapter 5

We bring Anni home

Cape Town, South Africa
Monday, November 15, 2010

At dinner that night Shrien was somehow still holding it together. He was managing to smile and chat away like everything was normal and nothing had happened. They say grief affects people in different ways and, right now, we were polar opposites.

I still could not find my appetite but Shrien coaxed me to order food and eat. An Indian family who were friends of the Dewanis had also joined us.

Shrien started talking more about what had happened that night. He had remembered there was a bump in the road as the kidnappers drove and how it had forced the car to jump upwards. He also recalled passing a green house. It was confusing. Earlier he had said he and Anni were forced to look down the whole time but I assumed he must still be in shock.

He also revealed to me for the first time that Anni had told him in Gujarati that she had put her diamond ring down the middle of the seat as they were kidnapped.

Then he returned to his food and his visitors.

As I surveyed the table I saw a group of people enjoying

their food and it seemed utterly surreal – as if we had all been invited for a dinner party, but it was still less than 24 hours since that horrendous phone call when they told me my Anni had been taken.

I was in a terrible state of grief. One guy, a stranger, came over and tried to comfort me. He talked about rape cases in South Africa and how horrific they had been for the victims. He told me about a tourist couple who had been attacked and taken to a mountain area. The man had been shot and the girl raped, before being cut into pieces. Her body parts were found in various areas. I know that deep down he was trying to make me feel better, but it had little effect on my grief. It just made me sadder – sorry for that couple and for South Africa in general.

Back in the lounge after dinner, Shrien returned to his laptop. After a while he looked up over the screen and told me he wanted to have Anni's funeral in England.

Naturally I said that was fine. I had no objection and agreed without hesitation.

In hindsight I wish I told him that I would have preferred to have had Anni's funeral in Mariestad where she had grown up and was so dearly loved. But it was not my call. Anni had been his wife, after all.

By now the strain was beginning to break me. My vision was blurred. My body was so weak I could hardly lift my arms or my legs. I felt as if I was in a bubble and it was a very lonely and cold place. When people spoke I heard echoes of their voices but was unable to take much of it in. Nothing, absolutely nothing, could have prepared me for this real nightmare.

I desperately wanted Nilam with me, beside me, along with my beautiful daughter Ami and my son Anish. I wanted Anni to walk through the doors of the hotel and hug me like she did when I left her in Mumbai after the wedding. I didn't want to be here in this room with these people. With nobody.

Prakash told me he and Shrien had been to the police station in Cape Town and had been informed they could not take Anni's body to Britain without a certificate from her doctors that showed she had no communicable disease.

I called my doctor Bengt Akerstrom in Sweden. He had known Anni since she was a baby and had travelled with his wife Inga to Mumbai to attend her wedding. He was a close family friend as well as our doctor. I explained the situation and he agreed to send a certificate immediately. It arrived by email shortly afterwards and was printed.

It is because of that we were allowed to leave the country so quickly. Once I had agreed with Shrien and Prakash about the funeral and presented the medical certificate from Sweden, I was asked to sign all sorts of official papers as her next of kin.

Although Shrien and Anni had been through a Hindu wedding ceremony, the civil ceremony which made it all legal had not taken place.

Finally I was to be allowed to see Anni. The police came to collect me from the Cape Grace at 3pm on November 15. I was told Anni was going to be taken on the same plane that Prakash, Shrien and I would be boarding back to London that evening.

I invited Shrien to accompany me to see Anni but he replied: "Dad, I can't come." Prakash told me Shrien should not go as it would make him too depressed. Prakash said that he would come with me to the police.

I was in tears the entire journey. What kind of event was this going to be? Surely, very difficult.

The morgue was en route to the airport. When we entered I saw Anni's coffin straight away and just stared at it. It was open and my daughter was lying there. Just like she was asleep. She looked so beautiful. I moved close to her.

I began wailing loudly and telling Anni: "Papa is here. I am so sorry. Papa is here."

I could not believe, in all my grief, that she did not get up to greet me. She lay there still in a red dress. Just still.

There was no sign of any injury to her, something I took some comfort from. At that stage I was not aware that she had been shot through her neck with a single bullet which had also pierced her hand. I would find this out later.

I kissed her on her forehead, telling her that I loved her so much, repeating: "Papa is here, Papa is here. I am so sorry. I have come to take you home."

The police officers and Prakash looked on as I began to ask: "How did this happen Anni? How?"

She looked like she was sleeping peacefully and might wake up and greet her father at any second.

A morgue is hard to describe. It's just such a horrible place to be and nothing can prepare you for it.

I could not remain standing for long. My legs were beginning to give way. It was all so unreal, but so very real. Nothing could have prepared me for those moments.

The police held my arm and advised that we should leave. But I could not take my eyes off my daughter's body. I wanted to have a few moments alone with Anni, but could not even muster the strength to make the request.

Before we left I asked Prakash to take a picture of Anni on my mobile as she was lying there. I really do not know why, because I certainly did not want to be remembering Anni like that. We said some prayers and blessed Anni to send her soul to heaven and let her rest in peace. That helped me a little bit.

I cried and sobbed like a baby on the way back to the Cape Grace, where I was surprised to hear Shrien tell us he had used the time to get a haircut and had bought a new suit.

I wondered if it would have been more decent of him to have accompanied us and paid his respects to Anni. But I had no intention of arguing, or even the will to reflect on it. I had been through a shocking episode and my energy was sapped. All I could think about was Anni and being back with my family.

Shrien did, however, try to explain his behaviour, telling me: "I am glad I didn't go with you because I would not be able to see her like that."

Later, as we sat around the hotel waiting to leave, I watched as Shrien was interviewed by two British journalists. I knew the murder of this beautiful woman on her honeymoon – my daughter – was a big news story. I could hear parts of the conversation between him and the journalists and wished I had the energy to listen in more closely as he offered them a detailed explanation of what had happened. I was still so desperate for information, for the facts – it was driving me crazy.

One of the British diplomats sat with us for some food before we left for the airport.

That's when the Dewanis opened up discussions about

the funeral, saying they had many relations in the UK who would want to attend as Anni had become part of their family through her marriage to Shrien. That was the reason it should be held in the UK, to give the Dewanis and their friends the chance to attend.

As her father I would have wanted greater involvement in the arrangements but I trusted them to organise it properly. Besides, I also had many relations in the UK and it seemed easier for my other family members to travel from Sweden.

I was amazed at the speed with which they worked and impressed that they had managed to sort out most of the arrangements by the time we were to leave for the airport.

We boarded a British Airways flight to Amsterdam at midnight and a connection to Bristol. I knew Anni would be on the same planes as ours but I didn't see her coffin being carried on. I didn't want to. I closed my eyes as I took my seat and tried not to look out of the window.

We took our business class seats. Me in the middle, Shrien on my left and Prakash on my right.

I thought about Anni being down there in the hold, how she was being transported with the luggage and it made my blood run cold. The immigration authorities had presented Anni's passport to me before we'd left. They'd stamped "Deceased" on the same page as her entry stamp at Johannesburg airport just nine days earlier when she had gone on a four day safari with Shrien before reaching Cape Town. There are no words in the English dictionary to describe the enormity of my pain.

Once we were in the air, Prakash ordered a whisky and I asked only for water. Prakash told me that I must have a whisky as it would make me feel better, but I couldn't drink.

He said a couple of drinks would make me sleep, but I knew nothing would work.

I was just thinking of my family and how they would take it when they saw Anni. I tried to talk to Shrien, but he needed to sleep. He opened his bag, took out his pyjamas, went to the toilet, changed into them, returned to his flat bed and slept while I sat there crying. I just wanted him to talk to me and tell me what happened.

At some point I must have dozed off too, although I awoke several times in tears and the air stewardess kept checking on me, trying to comfort me.

At Amsterdam we took a connecting flight to Bristol, where we landed at breakfast time. Shrien's brother Preyen had come to meet us. I was exhausted and we went to their house as the undertakers took Anni's body from the plane and to a chapel of rest.

When I went into their house I was surprised to see very large photos of Anni placed in big thick golden frames all over the house. I had never seen the pictures before. I recognised the wedding clothes and was shocked that they had all the pictures from Shrien and Anni's wedding so soon. I was under the impression that they had yet to come back from the photographer in India. The room was decorated with a lot of candles and flowers in a garland. Shrien's grandmother and his mother were crying a lot. I felt alone. I knew my family were on their way from London to Bristol and I could hardly wait for them to arrive so I could hug them.

My brother-in-law walked in that afternoon and held me tightly. It was what I needed. Nilam's other brother had travelled from his home in Brighton to help bring Nilam and other family members from Sweden for the funeral.

My brother in-law and I stayed a few hours with the Dewanis receiving mourners before he drove me to Brighton.

Later I deleted the picture of Anni in her coffin from my mobile phone as I didn't want Nilam or anyone else to see it.

I had only looked at it once more. But that was not how I was going to remember her.

Chapter 6

A surprise engagement

Mariestad, Sweden
Christmas, 2009

Months passed by since Anni's first visit home with Shrien. We did not see or really hear of him again. Meanwhile in Sweden a heavy winter had set in. It gets so cold that all you want to do is sit by the radiator and warm yourself. But my greatest warmth has always come from being surrounded by my family. Especially at Christmas.

It is a wonderful time in Máriestad, particularly when it snows and people go that extra mile to decorate the town in tinsel and fairy lights. We are not Christians but I am all for any excuse to bring my family together and enjoy their company.

There is something very special about Christmas, even if you are a Hindu or a non-Christian. There is a certain special kind of calmness that descends at the time and you cannot buy that kind of festive joy. It just happens.

That year, Christmas 2009, my two grandchildren came to visit from Stockholm with Ami and Henning so we could celebrate with the entire family. Just like we had done in previous years.

Anni loved Christmas. She was always the life and soul of the occasion, organising the party games and watching her niece and nephew open the presents she had bought. She always took great pleasure in spoiling them and repeatedly said she would have lots of children of her own once she had met the man she wanted to marry.

That Christmas she was not at home. Instead she spent it with Sneha and Anish in Singapore.

During this time, Anni did not mention Shrien much to me and I didn't want to interfere as I was unsure of the right thing to say. I felt that maybe she wanted to give the relationship a try without the pressures of parental interference. She certainly gave no indication of how the relationship was progressing, or floundering even, and Nilam and I agreed it was best not to ask.

It was only after Christmas and the New Year holidays were over, and the family had returned to their various locations around Europe, that Anni made one of her regular telephone calls to her mother.

That's when she announced she and Shrien were going strong and had become a couple.

She said he was a "nice guy" and that she had met his family and been accepted by them. Nilam and I thought this was all round good news and we kept our fingers crossed for Anni, who by now was 27.

I was happy though to receive a call soon after from Shrien's father Prakash, who introduced himself. He chatted away, telling me he was a pharmacist and his father Prabhudas had emigrated from Kenya to the UK, where he set up a business.

They now ran care homes for the elderly and Shrien and his brother Preyen helped run the business. There was also a third child, a daughter called Preyal.

Shrien, who had been born in Bristol, lived with him in the family home in Westbury-on-Trym.

Prakash seemed an amiable type and I took to him immediately. He kindly invited Nilam and me to visit them with Anni in Bristol and I agreed.

I worried later about whether it was the right thing to do or not as this was quite a step when we still didn't really know how serious the relationship was.

But, as if on cue, my daughter rang the very next day and said that it was a great idea to go there. Clearly the relationship had blossomed and I was worrying needlessly. I found myself telling her: "If you like him, go ahead."

I meant that she should put everything into the relationship and try to make it work with Shrien.

But later I thought about my words and felt I should have refrained from offering any advice and let the natural path of love take its course.

Anni was a lovely girl. Most men would fall for her beauty. Why, I asked myself, was I pushing forward her relationship with a man I hardly knew? I comforted myself that she was an intelligent young woman with a fierce streak of independence who would make up her own mind about any man she would spend the rest of her life with.

It was a beautiful sunny spring day in May when we made the journey over to the UK to meet the Dewanis. Instead of being invited directly to the family home, we were directed to the centre of Bristol to meet Shrien, who asked us to follow him in his BMW. His father feared we would have difficulty locating the flat they were staying in temporarily while their family mansion was renovated.

Nilam asked me to stop so that she could buy flowers for Shrien's mother Shila. She wanted to help create a good impression and bought a particularly beautiful bouquet.

When we arrived at the flat, Prakash greeted me with a traditional Namaste, I returned the gesture and we hugged. Over his shoulder I caught sight of a Pooja room, complete with deities, which I knew was a place to pray and I realised this was a god-fearing Hindu family.

Shila gratefully accepted the flowers and informed us that lunch was ready. Shrien's sister Preyal was on her way from London on the train. Shrien's brother Preyen and his wife were there too. It was looking like an important family summit.

It was a very palatable lunch, typically vegetarian prepared Gujarati style with dal, curry, roti and rice. I noticed that there wasn't much communication between Anni and Shrien, but I put that down to their respective parents being in the room and, perhaps, a touch of nervousness.

The lunch went well. It is always difficult to make an instant connection with people who were strangers to you a few hours ago. But Prakash and I got on and so did our wives. We chatted about Sweden, the weather in the UK, which is always a talking point, and the situation in India and Africa.

They informed us their main home had been under repair for more than a year, but they were hoping for the work to be completed by the summer.

The afternoon passed very quickly and then suddenly it was

time for tea in the garden in the marvellous sunshine.

I had felt very welcome and very comfortable but I was also on my best behaviour in the sense that I did not want to put my foot in it by saying the wrong thing. They always say that first impressions are lasting impressions and I listened attentively to the Dewanis' every word.

Prakash made Nilam and me feel very welcome and we took up his offer to have a look around the city in his car. We saw the Clifton suspension bridge, the Bristol Old Vic theatre and the cathedral. These were fine architectural structures and we liked the city, although when we walked we found some of the streets were very steep.

The Dewanis had booked us into the Hilton hotel and we went to freshen up before joining them for dinner at an Indian restaurant.

Once there, we had a nice surprise in that the owner was from my homeland in Uganda. Sadly, Nilam wasn't feeling well. She was still recovering from cancer and was feeling weak and tired. The travelling had been a bit much for her so we cut the evening short. Anni came back with us after we promised the Dewanis we would call in again in the morning.

Nilam and I chatted about the day and agreed it had gone well. We had not done anything wrong or said anything stupid which might make the Dewanis think less of our daughter. As I brushed my teeth I joked with Nilam that it was like an audition or having A-level pressure again.

We hadn't undergone this type of first meeting before. Our eldest daughter Ami had found her own husband without our help and she could not have chosen better.

Brunch at the Dewanis' home the next day was a rushed

affair as we were anxious to get back on the motorway to London and board our flights for Sweden.

The Dewanis were extraordinarily nice to us, showering us with compliments and repeatedly thanking us for visiting them. I thought they were such nice people.

It was so humbling to hear their kind words and to see the affection they gave Anni. Shrien and Anni had still not talked that much but I believed the youngsters were being respectful.

When the time came for us to leave, what happened left us, as well as Anni, absolutely shell-shocked.

Shrien's family presented us with a large silver dish, a thali, stuffed with fruits and nuts and with a bronze Ganesh statue placed in the middle. They congratulated us. This type of gift is traditionally presented in Hindu culture when a betrothal has been agreed between two parties.

Both Shrien's family and my own are religious and follow Hinduism as much as we can. It basically provides a structure or a backbone to live your life cleanly and respect others. So for something as pivotal as this to happen without any warning was shocking. Had I missed something?

We were confused as we had never even talked about an engagement with Anni, let alone with the Dewanis. Being the type of good-natured woman she is, and not wanting to risk offending our hosts, Nilam accepted the thali. She thought Anni must have known this was coming and didn't want to embarrass her in front of her future in-laws.

But I could see that she was also confused and taken aback. I don't think Anni understood fully what the underlying point of presenting the thali to us had been.

I was not adamantly opposed to Shrien marrying my

daughter but I would have liked to put the question to Anni first as to whether she thought she could spend the rest of her life with Shrien.

This was only my second meeting with the man who wanted to be my son-in-law and there are certain things any father would worry about. I was no different.

It was evident the Dewanis were not short of money and were all educated and upstanding people. But I wanted to be approached in the proper way by Shrien, not like this.

I was sure I wouldn't refuse a proposal to Anni from him, if that was what my daughter wanted. But meeting him twice was not enough and I would never have agreed to any marriage unless I knew the boy better and was sure that this was what Anni wanted.

On the way back to London the thali was respectfully placed on the spare seat and fastened under a seatbelt. It was the obvious topic of much conversation between us. None of us had seen it coming.

My daughter was engaged!

But Anni could not find a way to reject the proposal or engagement as she confirmed she had become quite close to Shrien over the preceding months.

I told her if she was happy to be engaged to him, then we as a family would have no problem with it and would support her.

I could see she wasn't convinced, just by the way she shrugged her shoulders. She didn't say very much as her mother and I discussed how we were shocked by the development.

We didn't know what was the right thing to say.

Then Anni simply said: "I like him… I don't love him… Oh, I don't know." She was as confused as we were about the whole situation.

Chapter 7

Emotions run high at the funeral

London, England
November 18, 2010

My family were finally all together. It was November 18 and we were in London to mourn Anni. It had been five days since my daughter was brutally murdered. I looked at my beloved Nilam. Words were not really necessary to ascertain how she was feeling. I then looked at my children, my brothers, my sisters, my nieces and nephews. We were in a state of absolute shock. There were so many tears. When we stopped crying we sat mostly in silence.

Occasionally we would share a memory of our Anni that raised a smile. But the smiles were quickly replaced by sadness as she was already being sorely missed and the fact that we would never see her again was establishing itself.

All the arrangements for the funeral were apparently finalised, although we received little information about what was happening and what was planned. My entire family was still in a state of extreme shock. But looking back now I realise that the funeral was too soon after my daughter's death. We wanted to plan the funeral for our beloved Anni as a family, or at least be a part of it. Instead we received invitations via

Facebook messages about where we should be and when we should attend.

I had heard that police back in Cape Town had arrested three men and one of them was the driver of the taxi that Anni had been shot in. A man called Zola Tongo. I wasn't as concerned with this development at this point, I was still too emotional to take it fully in. I had not slept properly for several nights and I was preparing to bury my daughter, something no father should go through. I would talk to the police once this weekend was over and, anyway, the media were already reporting the police breakthrough.

On the day before the cremation I received a phone call from Preyen informing me that Anni's body was at a funeral parlour in London. Apparently there was to be a pizza party later in the evening to give Anni a send-off. A what? A pizza party? I was so offended. How could my daughter's memory be honoured by a pizza?

Before this damned party we decided as a family that Ami and Sneha would go to the funeral parlour to dress Anni for the ceremony. I discovered later that Shrien also was there.

This is out of the ordinary in Hindu custom as only females are tasked with carrying out the dressing when a female dies. Similarly, when a man dies, males are tasked with preparing him for his funeral. It makes sense as it means the deceased's dignity is not jeopardised by being seen by a member of the opposite sex.

The dressing of Anni's body did not go well at all. It was already difficult enough but the girls informed me that Shrien threw a huge tantrum whilst there. Even his mother and aunty, who were also in attendance, looked shocked.

Ami was quite disturbed by the whole experience. She had never seen a dead person and that was difficult enough for her but this was her sister, her only sister. Understandably she had been a little scared to touch her. The room in the parlour felt cold. Anni was lying on a metal table. The body looked a little swollen but Ami later told me that Anni was still beautiful and looked peaceful as she lay there.

Ami had difficulty holding back her tears as Sneha helped dress Anni in a red sari and applied her make-up. It was exactly the way Anni would have wanted it. Sneha always used to do her make-up when the two girls were going out. That day was no different.

But apparently Shrien had been rough with Anni's body.

It was a particularly upsetting moment for Ami and Sneha when Shrien grabbed Anni's arm from Ami and dropped it down on to the metal table where she lay. Ami said she will never forget the "clunk" from the sound of Anni's arm crashing down.

Anni's body, frozen and embalmed, had swollen and Shrien forced the bangles which the girls had brought with them on to her hand, badly manhandling her.

Sneha pleaded with him: "Stop. You are hurting her."

Later, as Ami was standing by Anni's head, she asked him if it would be all right for Nilam and me to spend some time alone with her body a few minutes before the funeral, which was to take place the next morning.

Shrien said it was out of the question and told her: "You are not allowed to."

Shrien was in a hurry to get to his disrespectful pizza party as his father was collecting him at 6pm. When Sneha told him she would have to go home and take a shower first, he excelled himself in behaving disgracefully.

He asked her: "Why? Do you want to wash Anni off?"

To her credit Sneha hit back when she told him: "I will never wash Anni off."

But after everybody had left, Ami had the sense to turn her car around and drive back to the funeral parlour. She made a request to the manager, who said there would be no problem if Nilam and I, or indeed any other Hindocha family member, wanted to come 30 minutes before the funeral for a private farewell and some final time with Anni. I felt very hurt by this episode. I didn't understand why Shrien was behaving this way.

That evening the pizza party took place at the Kadwa Patidar Hall in Harrow. The name "Club 1740" on the invitation, I was told, referred to room 1740 at the Renaissance Hotel where the younger members of both families would gather to party in the days leading up to a wedding without the parents being around.

That was all about happier days and I took this to mean that Shrien wanted to evoke a similar atmosphere at his pizza party.

When we entered the hall it was nicely decorated with glowing candles. People were sitting on the floor singing bhajans and saying prayers. Many pizzas were passed around. But we Hindochas had, once again, lost our appetite.

The reason for the pizza party, Shrien explained to us, was because he and Anni had once attended a funeral where she had apparently said that if she were ever to die she would not want a sombre funeral but instead would like people "to eat pizza and chips".

That confused us as Anni had never liked chips. In Swedish chips means crisps which Anni used to love. Shrien simply must have misunderstood her.

There was a big screen in the middle of the room against a large wall with moving photographs of Anni and Shrien on a PowerPoint presentation created by Shrien. Pictures were shown from her childhood through to her wedding. I could not handle seeing the wedding pictures. The slides kept running on the big screen. There were barely any photos of my family, mostly photos of Anni and Shrien smiling together at the wedding. Seeing Anni smiling like that in her beautiful wedding dress just added to the pain and distress that I was already feeling.

I didn't feel that it was the right time or place to see such happy pictures and some of us broke down in tears. After all, she had been married only weeks earlier.

We were appalled and found the whole thing insensitive. We were in no fit state for this celebration. We sat smiling at the Dewanis and their friends but felt hurt and offended. Any proper tribute would have been decently restrained.

Ashok whispered to me: "They can't do this now. It is wrong."

Two of my cousins were so outraged they stayed in the hallway the entire time and hardly went inside at all.

It was just too soon and too lively. My daughter was to be cremated the very next morning and we were distressed thinking about it. Yet here were people tucking into pizza, drinking Coca-Cola, and it just felt wrong.

Sneha told me Shrien had confided in her: "We have to

make the funeral better than the wedding and make it really nice for her."

What perverse thinking was this? I either concealed my anger or was too broken to express my feelings. Or both. As I looked around at the people chatting amicably and tucking into their pizzas, I prayed the two hours would pass speedily.

It was irrelevant. Tomorrow was the day that truly mattered.

The next morning, around 20 members of the Hindocha family were granted permission by the funeral director to view Anni's body at a temple in Kenton before the service, after which she was to be transported to Golders Green Crematorium.

We arrived at 9.30am. Shrien was already there. This was to be our own family farewell to Anni and Ami asked him to give us our private time with her.

We were led through a corridor and into a very dull room with a blue carpet. Anni's coffin was open and placed in the middle of the room. Although her face was swollen, she was nicely dressed in her red sari. It was one of Nilam's that Anni had always wanted. She still looked so, so beautiful. Peaceful too, as if she were sleeping. I could not stop looking at her. I tried to hold it together but tears streamed down my face.

Ami and Anish along with all of her cousins had written letters to Anni and they placed them individually by her feet in the coffin. The family then stood in a circle around the casket, looking at Anni, and held hands.

My mother Ba, who was frail and in her eighties, was first to go up to the coffin and said something over her body before blessing her.

We took it in turn to approach Anni and say our own

goodbyes. It was a very solemn, quiet time. An important
spiritual few moments. I can still remember the melancholy
music playing in the background.

Ami was being as strong as she could, holding everything
together and ushering people forward. The feeling in the
room was very calm, very peaceful, and I felt as if Anni was
with us. We could all feel her presence in some way. This was
the first time I had ever a feeling like this and it comforted me.

Nilam, Ami and I were to be the last to say goodbye to Anni
and were not aware that 20 minutes had already passed when
Shrien burst in screaming.

He shouted: "What are you guys doing? You are not allowed
to do this."

My son-in-law of a few weeks insulted us by arrogantly
accusing us of being inconsiderate. Ami asked him to leave
but he refused.

Ami screamed at Preyen, who'd also entered the room, and
ordered him to get Shrien out. This intimate goodbye had
really been spoilt by this staggering intrusion on our private
grief.

Fortunately Preyen managed to calm down his
hysterical brother and got him out. But it took five minutes of
our valuable time. Ami asked everyone to leave so Nilam and I
could have a few moments to ourselves with Anni.

But as the other Hindochas left, Shrien re-emerged and
refused to budge. Ami asked Preyen once again to remove
him. I felt a pang of sympathy for him, thinking he had
become highly emotional because of the trauma of losing his
wife and the ensuing funeral, so I said that he could stay.

Ami, however, had had enough and ended up arguing with

Shrien. My nephew Neal had seen enough and asked in Swedish whether he should punch Shrien, but Ami managed to calm him down. All this while Anni was lying there.

After a couple of minutes, Shrien finally left. But precious moments had been lost and Nilam and I only had a few seconds with our daughter as the funeral was about to get under way.

I kissed Anni one last time, put my arm around my wife, and we left the room.

Ami never got her time to say a proper goodbye to her sister. Outside, her anger had turned to tears as she said: "Shrien took my final goodbye away from me. I never will forgive him. She was my sister. I had known her for 28 years. How could he do such a thing?"

Shrien had also refused to allow Anni's friends who had travelled from Sweden to view her body and had even tried to ban them from the funeral. I still put this bizarre behaviour down to him not being able to handle his grief.

But as we waited outside we saw strangers walking in with the Dewanis so we went back in and joined the back of the group.

Shrien placed four coconuts, considered in Hinduism to represent God, in the corners of the coffin and we all prayed.

He was the only one close to the coffin. All the other people kept their distance by a few metres as they sang the saddest songs.

But I was outraged when Ami pointed out that all the letters placed by the Hindochas in the coffin had been thrown out onto the floor.

Ami began berating Preyen about how this was allowed to

happen, telling him if they were not placed back inside the coffin she would scream the place down.

Thankfully, Preyen had the goodwill and sense to approach Shrien and force him to put them back. Emotions, understandably, were very heightened.

Then one of my nieces produced a bucket of red roses – a very sweet touch because Anni loved red roses. As Ami began handing them out to the Hindocha family, Shrien whispered something into his father's ear. Prakash announced: "Please respect that we do NOT want anyone to put any flowers in the coffin." Shrien then said: "I don't want her coffin to look like a dustbin."

So we stood there, each of the Hindochas holding one red rose in our hands. A red rose that was meant to be for Anni but was not allowed to be put next to her. Because of the problems going on around me, I was unable to get properly involved in any of the prayers. The Dewani family took control of the ceremony and it was soon over.

Later Preyen stepped in and persuaded his brother to stop this bullish behaviour and allow us to place the flowers. As the undertakers closed the coffin, we all cried for Anni. It was the last time I would see her face.

At least 150 mourners followed the coffin to the crematorium. Shrien had placed a wreath on the coffin and my family put a big heart of red roses on it with several notes of love from the Hindochas.

Before the coffin was placed in the furnace, Shrien said a few words in her memory and Ami read a poem. Prakash said a prayer, but such was my distress I could not bring myself to say any more.

As is traditional in our religion, we followed the coffin into the back room. People do not normally receive permission to enter the room where they actually burn the casket, but as Hindus we needed to see the cremation being carried out.

The coffin was placed in the furnace by two workers and, as they closed the door, we saw the flames rising and heard the sound of it being burned. Images and smells I will never forget.

Anni was no more and, as a family, we were broken.

Chapter 8

Anni has her doubts

Mariestad, Sweden
May, 2010

The day after we returned home from that first meeting with the Dewani family in Bristol, Nilam and I sat at the breakfast table with only one topic of discussion on the agenda. How had our daughter somehow got engaged without realising it herself?

As parents our natural default position was to worry. This situation was no exception. Anni had been dating Shrien on and off for almost a year now. Anni was insecure and didn't know what she wanted.

One day she would tell us that she wanted to marry him, and the next day she had her doubts again. For me, the important thing was to see my daughter happy. Whatever she decided I would be there by her side supporting her fully.

All sorts of things crossed our minds, one of the main being that we did not want to insult the Dewanis by asking for our daughter to be given some time to decide, properly and fully, whether she wanted to marry Shrien.

But still, Anni's bewilderment over the Dewanis' perception that she had agreed to marry Shrien bothered us because of

Anni not being completely sure of what she wanted. I just wanted the best for her and, as I mowed the lawn and Nilam looked out at me from the window, I could see my wife was as troubled as I was.

I began making a list of pros and cons in my mind. I started with the pluses. Shrien was good looking and he was well educated. He was a good Hindu boy and his family were very respectful. I was told by Prakash that they had even been honoured by the Queen, who had sent them a congratulatory message in 2006 for their care home work. Shrien would be able to support my daughter financially. To my mind, he was just like any other well brought-up boy who respected others.

Then came the negatives. Try as I might, I actually could not think of any. Even the fact that he had been engaged before and broken off the engagement was not enough reason to judge against him.

This was a man who was manifestly in love with my Anni. That love was transparent because why would he want to make her his wife if he was not determined to spend the rest of his days by her side? My only concern was that I didn't know him well enough. We had only met twice before, on Nilam's birthday and in Bristol.

But Anni's indecision kept bothering me. I decided I would phone her at noon London time, in order to give her the chance to relax properly and get some uninterrupted peace after what must also have been a stressful and draining 24 hours for her too. But I needed clarification from her, needed to know what she wanted.

I was going to call Anni and lovingly reassure her that I

would say whatever she wanted me to when I spoke with Shrien's family. She had to enter willingly into an engagement and all that would follow if that was what she wanted. But she could also walk away – with the assurance from her parents that she was making the right decision if that was how she felt.

We had to be quick to either confirm or reject before the wrong messages were sent out to Bristol.

It might be difficult for those outside the Hindu religion to comprehend, but avoiding the risk of violating the "izzat" or honour of both families was another issue I had to deal with.

I would not feel comfortable harming the Dewani family reputation any more than my own. But I did believe that I needed to square the issue of Anni's uncertainty about Shrien with his family as soon as possible, otherwise the whole thing could be very embarrassing. I was troubled that the Dewanis in their excitement might announce the engagement to their social circles.

It is a small world and their friends would probably know our friends in North West London, Leicester, Croydon and Brighton.

If word reached my family and friends that Anni had become engaged, it would cause a huge problem because right at the centre of it all was Anni's troubled response. She wasn't sure. The best scenario would be to discuss the situation together with Anni and give the Dewani family an honest response.

But Anni was still so uncertain and couldn't make up her mind up as to what she wanted to do and how she wanted to move forward together with Shrien.

Asking for more time for the proposal to be considered might give the impression that we were unsure about Shrien. As far as they were concerned, their son was going to marry my daughter. But my daughter was not going to marry their son. Well, not at this stage anyway. I didn't want her to take such a major step in her life when she was unsure.

I needed to be extremely diplomatic and neither cajole nor deter her from the marriage.

It was down to Anni.

Shrien's father was on the phone as soon as I entered the house and the tone of his entire conversation was as if everything had been agreed and it was all going to end with the marriage.

It was a conversation which would change all our lives.

Prakash is a softly spoken man and, at times, I had difficulty making out what he was saying. But I did hear him say that he and all the Dewanis were very happy that Anni was to be welcomed into the family and that he had decided to talk to his priest and receive his advice on the date for the wedding.

He wanted the priest to decide the date according to the Hindu calendar and tradition. In our religion, there are all sorts of spiritual and superstitious matters regarding important dates which, if I am truly honest, I do not fully understand. I feel many others are as confused by them as I am and we all just play along because the priest is regarded as never being wrong.

The call didn't last long and I found myself somehow giving the impression that it was agreed. Maybe I am too soft and try too hard to please.

I would give my life for my family, as I love all of them so much, but I don't like conflict and hardly ever raise my voice. I believe to gain a friend you have to be a friend first and foremost.

And there, in a call that could ultimately decide the future of Anni, I had not dared to declare my true thoughts, which were that we were getting a bit ahead of ourselves.

Nilam was absolutely understanding of my predicament and stressed that it was all down to Anni. Naturally, the next call was to her.

I explained what had happened since we had returned from the UK and that Mr Prakash Dewani was already talking about a date for her wedding. Anni responded with the words: "Papa, I don't know what to do."

Anni knew it was a big step and that she was uncertain. I knew it was a big step too. We discussed how long they had been dating and how they seemed suited and got on very well. She was hesitant and silent for a few seconds. I told her that whatever she decided she would have the full support of her parents. But I also told her: "Anni, I would be very happy if you decided to settle down but you have to do what you feel is right."

Those words came from a father who just wanted his daughter to find the perfect husband that would take care of her and love her for the beautiful person that she was. I wanted her to be happy. I had entered my sixties, her mother had suffered cancer and we just wanted her to be safe and feel comfortable.

Shrien ticked all the right boxes as far as we were concerned. It was a perfect match.

Chapter 9

A breakthrough in Cape Town

Stanmore, England
Sunday, November 21, 2010

A memorial service had been planned for Anni on Sunday, November 21. More than 1,500 people were due to attend and pay their final respects to her memory.

By now our entire family was running on empty. We were emotionally exhausted and Shrien's insulting behaviour at the funeral had drained us even further.

My family are not antagonists when it comes to arguments. We had found it very uncomfortable having to raise our voices and defend Anni's honour against the shocking onslaught Shrien had unleashed.

The time when we could return to Sweden, and when our relatives could go back to their own homes around the UK, could not come soon enough for us. Then we would be able to begin our own mourning process without interference from people we barely knew.

But Shrien had not finished with his mind games and his self-appointed position as mourner-in-chief. Now he even wanted to cancel the memorial for my lovely Anni. I had to seek an audience with him, literally beg him with both hands clasped as if in prayer not to cancel the event.

I didn't understand what was happening. Why would he want to do something like that?

Prakash had phoned me on Saturday evening saying Shrien was threatening to call off the memorial service completely, because he was angry. I was at a loss as to what I could have done to make him even angrier. Apparently the mourner-in-chief had been upset by Ami's behaviour at the funeral.

He suggested I phone Shrien and talk things over. So in an attempt to try to improve relations and stop the memorial service being called off, I contacted him and asked if we could meet to discuss the matter.

Shrien said the meeting could only last ten minutes and we were to meet at the VB & Sons store car park in Kingsbury.

Once there, I was surprised that he had still not calmed down. Shrien was imperious and rigid in response to my pleas. He demanded an apology from me before agreeing to go ahead with the memorial for my daughter. Of course I gave it. I wanted to keep the peace and I wanted to go to my daughter's memorial.

Shrien was evidently angered by Ami's rage at the funeral. I realised this was all about being in control. Ami had planned to say a few words at the memorial but he wouldn't let her speak at the service under any condition.

This was rapidly becoming a point-scoring exercise. Shrien was clearly not used to people standing up to him. But my kind, gentle Ami, whose nonsense threshold is lower than most in our family, had challenged him by arranging our own private time with Anni's body.

Whatever. None of it mattered. I still had to concede to Shrien's demands because I knew we had to do this. We wanted to do this. For Anni. If we were not allowed to speak at the service then at least we would be recognised by our presence.

It was embarrassing and utterly humiliating for me to be begging my son-in-law of a few weeks to attend my own daughter's memorial, but I felt I had no alternative.

The service went ahead at the Shree Swaminarayan Temple near Stanmore as scheduled. The hall was very large but nobody had decorated it. Chairs were put out in lines for people to sit. At the front there was a huge picture in a golden frame of Anni. We stood at the front together with Shrien's family. Everyone came to greet us and pass on their condolences before they took a seat. There was a long queue but the atmosphere was calm and respectful and everybody had a chance to come forward.

It was hard standing there. All these people. They were here because of Anni. I could not hold back my tears even though I tried so hard. When everyone had sat down we started with a prayer.

Ami was still smarting. After all, she'd not had the proper opportunity to say her goodbye at the funeral. She was still hurting, as we all were.

Ami had written a tribute to her sister and was going to make damn sure those attending heard her words.

She managed to bypass the ban on her speaking words of love to her sister by asking one of my cousins to read them for her.

Shrien began snarling as the words were read. But it did not deter my eldest daughter. I was proud of her as she and Anish walked from their seats and stood by my cousin Manoj as he read.

I imagine most of the 1,500 people simply thought Ami was too upset to read it herself. But she had scored a significant victory over the tyranny.

Throughout, Prakash sat on the edge of his chair. I could see he was contemplating getting up and perhaps putting a stop to the speech – his face seemed to be full of anger towards Manoj.

But Manoj went ahead and read what Ami had written:

"Family meant a lot to Anni. She cared a lot for us and always put her family first. She had several interests in life – sleeping, talking on the phone, eating good food, fashion and dressing up like a model. She knew how to dress up, so beautiful, graceful and always smiling our little princess was.

"Apart from her mum and dad, there were three people she loved the most. Her brother and sister and her absolute favourite cousin Sneha. She and Sneha were inseparable and did everything together always."

It went on to say how Sneha and Anni followed each other to study at the same universities and whenever they came home the first person they would seek out was always their grandmother Ba.

"Anni always made time for her friends and cared about them more than she cared about herself."

Ami added:

"You all knew Anni as beautiful, exciting and full of life. We knew her as stubborn, impulsive, inspiring and passionate.

"She was our little sister who was so generous with a heart of gold."

Ami recalled how Anni had moved in with Sneha in London and had met Shrien. She added:

"We all loved Anni so very much. She touched our hearts with her honesty and kindness. But look where we are today. Only two weeks after her marriage to Shrien we have lost her. We know that God has taken her because he always takes the best ones first.

"Wherever you are, our beloved Anni Hindocha, we pray that you are in a happy place, looking down on us and watching over us.

"You are now our angel and we will always keep you in our hearts."

People cried as the speech ended and Shrien ran out of the room. We managed to maintain our dignity for the rest of the event but it was hard.

Later Preyen phoned me and asked to meet at the same car park where I had previously been humiliated by Shrien.

There he urged me not to make public the text messages that Anni had sent to Sneha. I was confused. I wasn't clear why this was being asked of me, or even what these messages contained. But he asked me to keep the conversation just between us before offering to help me with anything I needed once I had returned to Sweden. I didn't really know what was going on but I thought that gesture was very decent of him. He hadn't needed to offer that and it touched me.

While Shrien's behaviour throughout the last week had offended me deeply, I received some breaking news from South Africa that instantly took my mind off him.

South Africa police's elite Hawks Investigation Unit had

detained three men as Anni's memorial was being conducted.

One, Xolile Mngeni, had been arrested on November 17. Two days later men called Mziwamadoda Qwabe and Zola Tongo, the taxi driver on the night Anni was killed, were also held. I didn't know how to feel when I heard the news. There was an element of relief but it was still too soon to feel anything other than intense grief.

All three men were charged with murdering Anni and aggravated robbery. The media in South Africa began running stories that Anni's murder had been a planned hit after a fourth man was detained. He turned out to be a hotel worker – Monde Mbolombo.

My information was that Mbolombo had acted as an intermediary between Tongo and the two kidnappers.

But there were also media reports that Tongo had turned state witness. I wasn't fully sure what the implications of this were but I understood he had begun helping the detectives. It was a confusing time for us all.

One of the British newspapers quoted a police source as saying that there was to be an "explosive revelation." I had no idea what this could be and instantly worried that they may have found new evidence that Anni had been assaulted before being shot.

There had also been a highly disturbing report about a student who said she was present when Anni was found. She claimed that Anni's underwear was around her knees and her dress pulled up to her waist. This caused me a great deal of distress before the police ruled this out as utter rubbish.

I've no doubt some people would wonder why I continued

to read so much, especially when a lot of it was untrue, or simply supposition. The fact is I was still desperate for information about what exactly had happened that night. Shrien still hadn't given me the answers.

Of course it was early on in the police investigation and there were sure to be many months before we got to a trial. I expected Shrien to be recalled to give evidence against the suspects. After all, he had been there.

But now there were messages reaching me from Cape Town that the police had begun to question Shrien's account of what happened. A so-called "friend" of the Dewani family told the newspapers that any suggestion that Shrien had been involved was "outrageous and disgusting." I honestly did not know what to think.

Meanwhile the police had recovered Anni's watch and two mobile telephones taken during the murder. Plus the gun used to shoot Anni had been found. The detectives appeared to be making progress and Shrien's name being mentioned in such questionable terms was something we would never have imagined.

Shrien's attitude and strange behaviour in the few days we had together in South Africa and now in London had concerned Sneha. His insulting arrogance regarding Anni's coffin was the final straw for her and she said she had to speak to us urgently

Sneha, ever loyal to Anni, had been keeping secret much of the edgy stuff that had been going on between my daughter and Shrien while they were in Mumbai for the wedding.

She called a family meeting while we were together in

London. Ashok, Anish, Ami and I then listened as Sneha revealed some worrying incidents between Anni and her groom in Mumbai which she said needed to be presented to the investigating officers.

It was absolutely the last thing on my mind that Shrien could be implicated in Anni's murder. She was his wife, murdered by a group of gangsters, and he had luckily escaped. But Sneha said the police would definitely be interested, at the very least, to know the background to the relationship.

She showed us a text message she had received from Anni on September 10, 2010, stating she wished that she had never got engaged to Shrien.

We also discussed a phone call I'd had from Shrien's grandmother in Mumbai on September 22, 2010, in which she informed me that Anni and Shrien had quarrelled.

Apparently Anni had taken off her engagement ring, thrown it at Shrien and informed him that she was no longer going to marry him as she stormed out of the hotel. At the time I had tried to contact Anni to substantiate what was going on but was unsuccessful.

I had believed the quarrels between Anni and Shrien were just trifling incidents caused by the stress of arranging such a big wedding. But the more Sneha disclosed, the more my concerns grew.

I listened as my niece talked about how Shrien had refused to be intimate with Anni. It was uncomfortable to hear. Sneha said he had attempted to have sex but there were problems. It made Anni believe he didn't find her attractive. I recalled her asking me if she was ugly. Was this why?

Sneha also said Shrien had criticised Anni's clothing and picked rows with her over nothing. He had even avoided sex on their wedding night.

One text message before the wedding from Anni had said: "I don't want to marry him. I'm going to be unhappy for the rest of my life. One cannot even hug him. We have nothing in common."

Another said: "Want to cry myself to death."

Sneha pointed out Anni had called off the wedding three times but each time Shrien had managed to persuade her to change her mind.

There had also been a problem when Anni had stayed with the Dewanis in Westbury-on-Trym, a few months before the trip to Mumbai.

She had sent a message to Sneha on August 5 which said: "Miss you so much. Don't want to be with these people. I don't know what to do. I'm much more comfortable alone. I hate them. Want to cry myself to death."

Later, on August 25, she had texted Sneha: "Feels very empty without you. Can't understand why I'm crying all the time."

Other text messages, revealed to me and my astonished family for the first time, read: "Crying every day… catastrophic and so much to do that I can't cope. I feel abandoned by everybody.

"Fighting a lot with Shrien. Told him I'm going home. Wish I never got engaged.

"Everyone tells me how fortunate I am. Even my designer

tells me that he's good-looking and that I am lucky. Absolutely sick. We're seeing each other for three days and only fight.

"I don't want to marry him. I'm going to be unhappy for the rest of my life. If I knew this I would not have got engaged.

"Do you think I will be able to find someone else if I break this? Feels bad that everyone has booked their tickets.

"I'm not happy. One cannot even hug him. We have nothing in common. He is putting pressure on everything.

"He's a perfectionist. Don't want to, but I feel sorry for my parents."

I was stunned at the messages. I listened in horror at how my little girl had poured her heart out to her cousin during the build-up to her wedding.

Sneha showed us more text messages which said: "We are going to sort everything out but I still feel the same way." Anni also said she hated Shrien: "Hate him. I am not happy." She talked several times about divorce.

Anni also told Sneha that Shrien had booked a surprise visit to South Africa but his mother had let her know about it by mistake. Anni had informed Sneha: "I don't want to go anywhere with him."

It only made me feel sadder.

By now, such was the media interest in the case that Shrien himself went on record denying any involvement in Anni's death. "How could anyone say I killed her?" he asked, adding: "Losing Anni was the end of my world."

He went on: "I feel like I have been robbed of the rest of my life. I had searched high and low for my perfect partner.

Anni was the one – her looks, her laughter, her personality, her spirit. Everything about her was right for me. Why should I want to kill her? Saying I was somehow involved seems to defy logic. I can't bear to think about her last moments and what she must have been through with those men but I know she loved me and she must have been thinking of me."

In another interview Shrien, who by now had been requested by the police to return to Cape Town to identify the suspects in an ID parade, even talked about his affection for Tongo.

I read that he had said: "I had a lot of suspicion about the driver. But he helped the police and was able to answer all the police's questions. By the end of it, I quite liked him."

Such was the interest by now in the case that Preyen asked me to accompany him to the office of the British publicist Max Clifford in Mayfair, London. At that time I had no idea who Max Clifford was. I had never heard of the name before and I was very unaware of why we were there.

Clifford wasn't there but Preyen took out his mobile, put it on the table and I saw that he was recording something.

He asked me: "Do you like your son-in-law?"

"Of course I like him," I said.

Shortly afterwards, a headline appeared in a national newspaper, promoted by Clifford of course, which read:

"Father-in-law loves son-in-law like his own son."

I was not media savvy enough to understand that a public relations battle to keep Shrien's name clean was beginning. I later felt I had been unwittingly drawn into it.

For a start, I never said I loved him. I said I liked him and

I think the fact that I said "of course" was more to challenge the absurdity of the question rather than a comprehensive statement of any affection for Shrien.

Yes, he had been a troublemaker at Anni's funeral and I had found out he had, at times, made her life miserable in the time leading up to the wedding.

But I still found no reason to speak out against him, so when I was asked the question by his brother, I answered it as honestly as I could. He was my son-in-law and I responded to the question honestly.

Preyen also asked me to sign a statement attesting to the strength of my feelings for Shrien but I refused.

I had been used. I had been quite shamelessly used to promote a client by Clifford, who as I write is in jail for sexual assault. Clifford's normal business involved kiss-and-tell ventures in tabloid newspapers. What was he doing being invited and paid to interfere in a murder case?

I met Shrien once more at his family's flat near Marble Arch with Nilam and Sneha.

He was upset and cried a lot. He talked us through some more details of what had happened the evening that Anni died. However, he now changed his version from the first time we had spoken.

Now he alleged that the driver had inquired if they wanted to see "real African dancing." He had previously stated that that Anni had insisted on going to see the "real African nightlife." It was very confusing.

I told him I planned to collect Anni's clothes from their house in Bristol. He asked that I leave the Christian Dior

shoes and the black Karen Millen dress he had bought for
her when they got engaged so that he had something to
remember her by. I agreed.

That night we drove to Bristol and back, very tired and very
muddled about what was going on. We collected Anni's
clothing and also some jewellery we had given her as wedding
presents.

I could not stay in London any longer and Nilam and I flew
back to Sweden early next morning before breakfast time.

In Mariestad we were unable to settle and begin the
mourning process for Anni with so much focus falling on
Shrien. The reporters from London arrived in my hometown
and, although I had never spoken to the media before, I could
only be honest and try to help them.

I relayed my despair at the sudden turn of events. But
I could not give them any new information about the
investigation.

My family, extremely unhappy with the memorial service
arranged by Shrien, held their own in Mariestad which was
attended by around 500 people who really knew and loved
her. My sister-in-law Nisha did a wonderful job decorating the
hall with candles and photographs of Anni.

Shrien was not invited. It would probably be fair to say he
was not even considered for an invitation. Yes, he had been
her husband, but he had been very hurtful and disrespectful
to our family.

This time Ami was able to express her feelings without
being prevented. She spoke, along with Anni's cousins, about
this wonderful young woman's short life.

There was a PowerPoint presentation again, only this time it contained photographs of Anni as a child and as a young woman, with none from the short and ill-forsaken marriage.

Unfortunately, Ashok and I were unable to attend the Hindocha family service for Anni. I had taken a call from Lieutenant Colonel Mike Barkhuizen of the South African police. He said he needed me back in Cape Town and would tell me what had been established when I got there.

I left immediately.

Left: Anni, on the right, with her big sister Ami. They were always very close despite the five year age gap. Anni would have been about one at the time.

Below: Anni was three when this picture was taken. It is one of our favourites.

Right: When Anni was at school she wrote a book in Swedish entitled: Book about myself. It had some very sweet hopes and dreams for her life, including meeting her Prince Charming, which she revealed in her own writing.

I built a wooden deck outside our home so Anni could sit there and enjoy the sun.

Anni went to study at the University of Gävle. We were very proud of her.

Cousins Sneha and Anni had grown up together, having been born a year apart, and were like the two proverbial peas in a pod.

Above: Ami and Anni at a wedding in Mariestad, Sweden.
I could not have been prouder of my two beautiful daughters.

This picture of Anni and me was taken at a surprise party for me on my birthday.

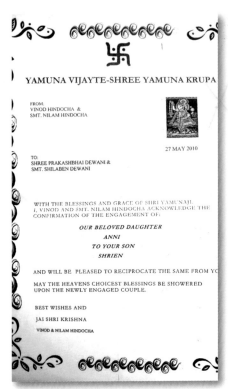

YAMUNA VIJAYTE-SHREE YAMUNA KRUPA

FROM:
VINOD HINDOCHA &
SMT. NILAM HINDOCHA

27 MAY 2010

TO:
SHREE PRAKASHBHAI DEWANI &
SMT. SHILABEN DEWANI

WITH THE BLESSINGS AND GRACE OF SHRI YAMUNAJI,
I, VINOD AND SMT. NILAM HINDOCHA ACKNOWLEDGE THE
CONFIRMATION OF THE ENGAGEMENT OF:

OUR BELOVED DAUGHTER

ANNI

TO YOUR SON

SHRIEN

AND WILL BE PLEASED TO RECIPROCATE THE SAME FROM YO

MAY THE HEAVENS CHOICEST BLESSINGS BE SHOWERED
UPON THE NEWLY ENGAGED COUPLE.

BEST WISHES AND

JAI SHRI KRISHNA

VINOD & NILAM HINDOCHA

Above: Anni looking radiant.

Above: The Hindocha family confirms the engagement in the conventional Hindu way – by exchanging formal statements.
Below: Nilam, Anni and I at the mandvo ceremony in Mumbai.

Anni at the chundari
ceremony in Mumbai.

Above: Mendhi artists
decorate the arms
of the bride.

Left: Anni performs
a dance at the
mendhi ceremony.

Top left: The wedding mandap that Anni designed herself. *Top right:* The reception venue. *Bottom left:* The entrance to the mendhi venue. *Bottom right:* The entrance to the chundari ceremony.

Above: Anni being carried to the mandap with family members including Ashok (left corner). *Right:* Myself, Nilam, Anish and Anni at the mandvo ceremony.

Above: I wanted to give Anni the dream wedding she had hoped for.

During the three days of ceremonies and the formal Hindu marriage ritual in Mumbai we witnessed three months of Anni's creativity come to life. It was her big occasion and she clearly wanted it to be memorable for her as well as every guest who attended.

She looked incredible throughout. Majestic. Like a princess.

Right: Anni and Shrien's wedding portrait was meant to be shared amongst friends and family as a memento of that happy day. But instead it has been shared with the world for such a different reason, a bitter symbol of the loss we will always feel.

Chapter 10

The wedding is on

Mariestad, Sweden
Easter, 2010

We talked a lot with Anni about the engagement in the days following that Easter Bank Holiday weekend in Bristol. Each and every day since the discussion with the Dewanis on April 5 we mulled over the situation between ourselves, as well as with Anni.

Sometimes she leaned towards an acceptance but at others she would revert back to statements such as: "But I don't know him very well."

While all this was going on I lived in hope that the Dewanis would not call to update me on the wedding planning that was undoubtedly going through the early stages. I even decided to leave my phone on voicemail and return any calls later to avoid Prakash telephoning about the wedding.

In the meantime I called my aunt in Kenya because I'd heard from some family members in the UK that she had known the Dewanis for more than 40 years. She said they were a good family, which was a huge step forward and made me feel more positive. I was informed that Shrien had an economics degree from the University of Manchester and had been general secretary of the National Hindu Students Forum there. Sounded good.

But it didn't matter how well educated he was, or how good a man. It didn't matter what I thought. It was still down to Anni to decide what she wanted to do. But I was glad that she and Shrien were continuing to see each other during this time, raising my hopes that she would work it out for herself.

One night in early May when I was having difficulty sleeping – it stays light until such a late hour and the sun rises so early at that time of the year in Sweden – Anni called. She wanted to tell me some news. She'd decided she was going to marry Shrien after all.

Prakash and I were soon on the phone at least two or three times a day, discussing how best to formalise the engagement and make the announcement. There was also the actual wedding date to be fixed. It is always a question of honour and a bond between the two families involved to agree the betrothal publicly.

We decided to announce and confirm the engagement in the conventional Hindu way by exchanging formal statements. These are not legally binding but bring to bear a kind of moral pressure on both parties to perform the wedding under the full gaze of family, friends and other well-wishers, and to do so with full Hindu custom being observed. The announcements were exchanged on May 27, 2010.

I was quite surprised to find the Dewanis had made a rather bigger show of the announcement, listing their son Preyen as top of their official confirmers, followed by his wife Kripa and Shrien's sister Preyal.

I had listed just myself and Nilam. The wedding had to be about my daughter and her special day. Most importantly, it was official now and we were all excited to start planning the wedding.

Anni had told me that she hoped that Shrien would propose the old traditional way to her. I am an old romantic at heart and so I was delighted when Anni told me that Shrien sealed his bid to make Anni his bride when he flew her to Paris and formally asked her to marry him at the Ritz Hotel on June 10, 2010. He had presented her with a stunning diamond engagement ring over dinner in a private area. The ring had been delivered on a plate instead of the dessert.

Not many women would have been able to ignore such a charming gesture. It was the ideal proposal for my romantic Anni and she fell for it. My daughter's heart had been won over in the most perfect fashion.

On her return from Paris she sent a Facebook message to one of her cousins in which she said of Shrien: "Damn I really like him now. I am in love!!! :))) It is his personality, he makes me so happy and laugh all the time and I cannot be without him. So I will give it all a chance now!!! :))) … hope to see you soon we really had so much fun together… YOUR BROTHER-IN-LAW maybe…"

In a second Facebook message to one of her cousins she said: "Please say that we can meet up. You have to see my ring!!! Between me and Shrien it's all going very well, we are travelling to Dubai 2 July so make plans for a wedding on 18,19, 20 Nov in Dubai.

"He is very nice and I really feel that its right (for the first time). I want to meet you and hug and talk."

Anni said she had known nothing about the trip to Paris until she boarded a private plane. Sneha had played Cupid by somehow smuggling Anni's passport to Shrien.

Anni was so happy and excited and couldn't wait to tell the family and all her friends. The bride-to-be spoke so fast I had to slow her down. I was so happy I cried and Nilam had to take the phone off me.

After that, things moved very quickly. Everybody appeared happy and, understandably, the good news spread fast.

Both Anni and her fiancé were keen on the wedding taking place in Dubai because of the sunshine and the grand way they do things over there. I felt no reason to disagree, purely because I wanted Anni's big day to be the most perfect and special one possible.

Within weeks, Shrien and Anni travelled to Dubai to have a look at possible venues.

While they were there, Shrien's father called and asked if we would agree on the wedding taking place in the late autumn – probably October or November – as Preyen's wife was pregnant with their first child and the birth was expected to be in the New Year. I said any date was fine with me.

Anni, who was renowned for being fairly impulsive, also called from Dubai. She and Shrien were now travelling to India to do some shopping for their big day. Once they got there, the couple changed their minds about the wedding venue. They no longer wanted the wedding in Dubai. They wanted to be married in Mumbai.

Anni told me: "Papa, I feel more at home in India."

I readily agreed, so pleased to hear how excited she was.

Shrien and Anni chose the Renaissance Hotel at Powai in

Mumbai, India's film city. They had studied magazines, checked the internet and sought the advice of close friends and family. Anni reassured me that if I found it too expensive she would not be upset.

That was never going to be the situation surrounding my daughter's wedding. I was determined to give her the best and nothing less. The same went for Shrien, who I would regard as my son and shower with love.

I had worked hard and saved all my life for the weddings of my two daughters. There was no point in keeping the money in reserve for anything else. As I grow older I need fewer possessions and, although the tax rates in Sweden are painfully high, I can still garner a reasonable income and live comfortably.

I checked my bank accounts and looked at flight costs for the large Hindocha family, the cost of the hotels and the actual wedding, and I wasn't concerned. Sure, it was going to be the biggest layout of my life. But it was Anni's big day. It had to be the best day of her life thus far. One that she and Shrien and eventually, her children, would talk about for years and years. The best, nothing less, and just the way Anni wanted it.

Shrien's father and I agreed how the costs should be shared, deciding that two thirds would be met by me and a third by him. As the bride's family we would pay for the three ceremonies that we wanted, while the Dewanis would pay for the fourth and their own reception after the union had been made official. Prakash said that we shouldn't get into figures just yet but that Preyen would let me know what my bill was to be. I was more than happy with that.

Something which did concern me, however, were the

rumours that there were issues between Shrien and Anni – at what was supposed to be the happiest time in their lives. I could not quite understand what the problems were.

I heard that Anni had been describing him to Sneha as "a Hitler." After one particular row she told him not to regard her as a possession, threatening to leave him and return to Sweden.

Anni was accusing Shrien of trying to control her. He was suffocating her with his stringent monitoring of her whereabouts and her everyday life. Anni was a free spirit and had been brought up with the utmost freedom to do as she pleased. Both Nilam and I trusted that she would never deliberately embarrass us, and she had never been known for overspending.

There were times when I would gently tick her off for buying expensive gifts, but that was the type of kind-hearted girl she was. But she was never wasteful, greedy or self-indulgent.

More worryingly, Anni had confided in her cousins that Shrien had asked her to provide him with a monthly Excel spreadsheet of her spending. He wanted to keep a check on what she was buying and felt he should monitor the amount she spent.

This was ridiculous. Anni was never an over-spender and yet here was the man she intended to marry ordering her, business-like, to keep a record of her spending and update him on a Microsoft Excel document. What happened to plain, simple romance?

I also heard that, in addition to watching her expenditure, Shrien wanted her to fold her clothes away each night like he did and to keep everything tidy. He even folded his own dirty

T-shirts and underpants in the laundry bag.

Another time, Shrien had reprimanded Anni for carrying her items in a plastic bag in London's Oxford Street and accused her of "acting like a tramp." The manufacture and material of the bag had embarrassed Shrien.

He was becoming very controlling and treating her like a child.

Of course I was curious when I heard these stories, but not enough for me to be suspicious of the man who was going to marry my precious Anni. At the end of the day, the couple always gave me the impression that all was well between them as they forged ahead with the wedding arrangements.

It was at the back of my mind, and is probably at the back of the minds of most fathers who are about to see their daughters married, that maybe this man might break her heart, use and abuse her or even jilt her at the altar. He could easily have been one of those types who tells a girl he loves her until she succumbs and falls into bed with him, only for the girl to be left stranded.

But Anni, who'd had previous boyfriends and was brought up in the West, wasn't naïve. Besides, Shrien evidently wanted to marry Anni. This was comforting and helped remove the small doubts over his strange behaviour from my mind. I thought Anni was safe with him.

More information came my way. In hindsight I wish I had taken more seriously the few times that Anni tried to share with me her worries about Shrien's lack of passion.

On one occasion Anni actually asked me: "Am I ugly? Aren't I good looking?" It is hard for any father to think about what his daughter is getting up to with a man and I was no different. It is extremely difficult for a father to discuss his daughter's love life, particularly with her. I suppose I did not want to cross the line.

Subconsciously, perhaps, I wanted to move away from the subject and so I told her that it was probably because they were both so tense with all the marriage planning and the work to be done.

I'd already heard, before the engagement had even been announced, that Shrien had health problems. He'd told Anni he was receiving hormone treatment for infertility. He had also told her he had travelled to Thailand for a Thai boxing course which he believed would raise his hormone level. He claimed this had been successful.

I always believe the best in people and I thought that as Shrien had been brave enough to tell Anni about his infertility problems then he has no reason to lie about the treatment. After sharing this with her prior to the wedding, I saw no reason for him to lie.

Much of this had gone on before the engagement and I believed the surfacing of the earlier tensions and the rows and disagreements were surely down to the pressure of organising the wedding.

It was to be the biggest day of their lives and Anni was determined to have every aspect of the ceremonies detailed and fail-safe.

I just put all these problems down to pre-wedding nerves and having to be the focus of attention for so many people from two large families.

Anni was intelligent, vivacious, caring and so, so beautiful… a wonderful woman who would fascinate most men. I was certain the rows would blow over.

Shrien was a lucky man to be marrying my girl.

Chapter 11

The police suspect Shrien

Cape Town, South Africa
December, 2010

The allegation was revealed to me perfectly calmly. Yet it was still incredibly painful and utterly shocking when it was confirmed and voiced out loud by the authorities.

Ashok and I had arrived in Cape Town with my brother-in-law Bharat to be met by police. We were immediately taken straight to the offices of Rodney de Kock, Cape Town's Director of Public Prosecutions.

Two senior police officers, Lieutenant Colonel Mike Barkhuizen and Captain Paul Hendrikse, also joined us to discuss the developments in the case since I had left South Africa with Anni's body.

Mr de Kock, a man of small frame but incredible confidence and experience, accused Shrien of paying to have Anni murdered. His theory was that Shrien had enlisted Zola Tongo to help stage the hijacking of the taxi and two killers had been hired to shoot her.

Tongo had gone through a hotel worker who had brought in Xolile Mngeni and Mziwamadoda Qwabe, two local gangsters, to carry out the murder.

Tongo and Qwabe had already appeared in court by the time we arrived in South Africa. The South Africans were considering allowing Tongo to enter into a plea bargain whereby he would receive a reduced sentence if he pleaded guilty and explained everything about how the murder took place.

I sat there, my lips trembling and tears rolling down my face, as Mr de Kock told me the astonishing story of how he believed Shrien had organised Anni's murder. He said the investigation was at an early stage but his officers were hoping to have the full facts within weeks.

Tongo had offered to turn state witness but, in any case, had made a full confession and implicated my son-in-law.

"I know this is very difficult for you, Vinod," said Mr de Kock, "but we are going to need you to be as strong as you can and to give us as much information and time as possible."

I had so many questions to ask him and he answered what he could – but there was still so much I didn't know.

He said he believed Shrien had employed Tongo in a chance meeting outside Cape Town airport when the driver took them to the Cape Grace Hotel in his car.

Shrien had been in touch with Tongo several times during that day and the next, and the driver had met the killers on the morning of the day Anni was to have been murdered.

Tongo and Shrien, it was claimed, agreed a plan whereby the newlyweds would be driven through Gugulethu and the two hired assassins would stop and hijack the taxi.

Both Shrien and Tongo would be released and then Anni would be murdered. Shrien and Anni were to be stripped of their valuables to make the robbery look real instead of faked.

I was utterly astonished to hear Mr de Kock say that Tongo had visited Shrien at the Cape Grace to collect part of his payment for helping stage the hit at the same time I was there during the few days after the shooting. I could not get my head around any of it. Police said they had made a mistake in allowing Shrien to leave South Africa so soon after Anni's murder, but at that stage he was not a suspect and it looked like a chance attack.

Understandably I agreed to stay on in Cape Town and help the police as much as I could.

By now the case had become front page news in both South Africa and the UK, although it went largely ignored by the Swedish media in comparison.

TV news bulletins were featuring Anni's picture looking beautiful in her wedding sari. It was an image that was starting to become pretty iconic.

I used to think about the many other sad cases of women being murdered around the world, and somehow Anni had become a daughter of the world. Her life and death had resonated far beyond what I could ever have imagined.

Even at the airport I had seen her face on TV screens and I was told Cape Town police were receiving requests from the media for information from all quarters of the globe.

My family in London told me both Shrien and his brother Preyen had gone on record to deny his involvement.

Preyen was reported to have told the media that his sibling believed he was being wrongly accused to save the reputation of South Africa.

I was annoyed when I learned that Preyen had been quoted denying a rift between me and Shrien, further repeating the claim that I had said I loved Shrien.

Preyen was said to have declared: "Both the Dewani and the Hindocha family want to see justice done. Anni's father has again said he loves Shrien like a son."

Max Clifford, the publicist, continued to take the Dewani money and pontificate on the case to media. I still could not understand why the Dewanis had employed him to represent them on such a serious matter and I was deeply offended.

Back in London, Clifford said of Shrien, "I have met him. I have spoken with him. I have looked him in the eye. I have talked it through. I have asked him all the questions that journalists have been asking and all circumstances and I totally believe him."

So that was OK then? Dewani was innocent, says Max Clifford, the self-appointed judge and jury.

As long as the Dewanis' paid publicist had pronounced Shrien innocent, then there was no need for the South Africans to pursue their case against him or at least bother talking to him. Insult after insult. He may well have been innocent but this individual was beginning to grate.

I knew I had to keep my mind focused on the case against the three accused men and help the police with as much background on Shrien as possible when the request came, which I knew it would.

Right now, Ashok and I had a tough question to face: should we allow Zola Tongo to receive a lesser sentence if he agreed to help the state in its case against the two arrested men and Shrien?

Mr de Kock told me that, as Anni had not been legally married to Shrien and the ceremony they went through had not been registered as such, I was recognised as her next-of-kin.

That meant, under South African law, as the blood relative of the victim, I had a say in whether Tongo would be allowed out of jail sooner than he would normally. The court would need my approval and I would have to sign acceptance of the plea bargain before it could be lodged before the court.

I had a lot to consider. If this Tongo had brought about the murder of Anni, then he deserved to be locked away for ever and the key thrown into the sea. In my eyes he had been responsible for taking Anni to her death.

Why should I afford him the luxury of leaving his prison cell as a reward? It was difficult not to be angry, but grief and common sense were the winners.

Ashok and I discussed the options for many hours before we agreed that acceding to the National Prosecution Authority's request was the sensible thing to do. I hadn't even given the case against Shrien much thought at that stage as things were moving so rapidly. It was hard to sit and take stock of it all.

Once the plea agreement was signed by me, I called my family in Mariestad. I knew they were eagerly awaiting news from Cape Town. I told Anish to inform the rest of the family that there was about to be a huge media revelation, that I wasn't able to say much more but that they should follow the news. Shortly after, it was revealed that Tongo claimed Shrien had hired him to plot a fake carjacking for the murder of his wife.

In Bristol, Shrien was arrested at a local police station after surrendering himself to officers there.

An arrest warrant was issued in London and delivered to

Bristol by Scotland Yard officers who sped down the M4.
They first called to arrest Shrien at the Dewani home in
Marble Arch. But Preyen's wife had told them he wasn't there.
Word reached Shrien at Westbury-on-Trym and he gave
himself up rather than having detectives call at his family
home.

South African police told me Preyen actually asked their
British colleagues if it was necessary for his brother to spend
the night in the police cells. He was told Shrien was a murder
suspect and it was absolutely necessary.

I had been appalled at Shrien's behaviour at Anni's funeral
and for the unkind way he had treated my family and me. But
I was careful not to let it colour my judgement against him.
Disliking someone's antics during an emotional period does
not make them a murderer.

I lost many hours of sleep night-after-night over whether my
son-in-law could have murdered Anni. It was a nightmare for
all the Hindocha family.

Effectively what the police were saying was that we had
married Anni off to a killer who took her life less than two
weeks after he became her husband.

For me, after Anni's death, if this allegation was true, it was
the biggest disaster we could face. I know that 99.999 per cent
of fathers would give their lives for their daughters. Instead,
had I been responsible for endangering her?

If Shrien was implicit in Anni's death then the fault also
lay at my feet. How could I have let my daughter marry
somebody who belittled her and insulted her both in life and
in death? Why had I not stopped this union?

Anni was unhappy and I had not been able to read the signs.

I'd hoped that they would work it out.

Now she was dead and her husband stood accused of organising her murder.

He had to face justice and he had to answer the questions. But all I could think about each night as I went to bed in Cape Town was how sorry I was. I prayed for forgiveness from Anni in heaven every evening. I was so, so sorry.

On December 7, 2010, Tongo appeared before Judge President John Hlophe, who was told by Mr de Kock that Anni "was murdered at the insistence of her husband."

Ashok, Bharat and I sat in front of Tongo as he appeared in the dock. I clutched a large photograph of Anni and sobbed the whole way through the hearing. It was so hard to listen to everything that was read out. My heart ached and I kept thinking of Anni. My poor little Anni.

Tongo, in his own words, told the court: "After we arrived at the hotel, Shrien Dewani approached me alone and asked me if I knew anyone that could 'have a client of his taken off the scene.' After some discussion with him I understood that he wanted someone, a woman, killed.

"We would make it appear as if we were the victims of a random armed hijacking of my motor vehicle, committed with a firearm. The hijacking would be simulated.

"The kidnapping and robbery were part of the plan to make it appear that this was a random criminal act, unconnected to Shrien Dewani.

"He said he was willing to pay an amount of 15,000 rand."

Tongo, who bowed his head for much of the time and refused to make eye contact with me, admitted he had spoken with a middle man (Mbolombo) and then been put in touch

with Mngeni and Qwabe. He said he met them the following
day to arrange Anni's murder.

When he picked up Anni and Shrien he took them to a
restaurant where Shrien told him he wanted my daughter
killed that evening.

I felt sick and close to collapse as Tongo's words filled the
courtroom describing Anni's last few hours. I had wanted to
know this information so much. Now I could hardly bear to
listen to it.

He said he took them to the prearranged hijack spot, an
intersection in Gugulethu, where the attackers entered the
vehicle, a VW Sharan.

Tongo went on: "The Dewanis were made to lie down on
the back seat and Qwabe drove off.

"Qwabe travelled for a short distance before he stopped
near the police barracks in Gugulethu, where I was ordered to
get out of the vehicle.

"I knew that Mngeni and Qwabe would not harm Shrien
Dewani and that he would be dropped off at some further
point. I also knew that the deceased would be kidnapped,
robbed and murdered by Qwabe and Mngeni."

Anni's body was found in Tongo's car near Sinqolanthi
Street, Ilitha Park, Khayelitsha. She had been shot through
the hand and neck and the bullet had damaged her spine.

These were the words of a man who had arranged my
daughter's death, spoken without any compassion, similar to
the way he had led Anni to her murder.

I felt so much anger inside of me I could start screaming.

But my dignity remained intact in front of the large number
of journalists who occupied the press seats.

Because of my agreement, I had effectively given Tongo seven years off his sentence. He received 18 years instead of the 25 which was the expected and recommended sentence. But I could never forgive him. I would never forgive him. That night I saw on the news that Shrien's family had issued a statement that he was "totally innocent of any involvement in this heinous crime."

I realised the attention would soon turn to him now that the first of the three arrested men had been put away.

It wasn't my place to decide whether Shrien was involved or not. That was up to a court of law and I fully respect the due process of the legal systems. It was up to the police to establish a motive and to prove guilt or for the court to find him innocent.

But it was my right to demand that he came to South Africa and gave me and a judge the full story. He owed me that at the very least.

I did tell reporters as I left the court room: "We are very, very confident about the police investigation."

Photographs of me which accompanied the front page reports the next day, clutching Anni's photograph with tears in my eyes, caused further distress back at home. But I could not help myself. I was inconsolable.

Sadness was replaced by frustration later that night when I saw that Max Clifford surface once again to talk about Anni.

He told a TV interviewer that Tongo should be treated with contempt. He went on to reveal Shrien was grieving and receiving trauma counselling.

Police reassured me that it was only a matter of time before Shrien was put back on to a plane to Cape Town to face questioning.

Nobody told me that particular "matter of time" would be a sentence in itself for all members of the Hindocha family.

It was to prove to be a long wait.

Chapter 12

Wedding plans

Mariestad, Sweden
October, 2010

Despite any misgivings we may all have had about the unusual engagement, we all embraced the wedding planning. This was for Anni, and we just wanted the best for her and for her to be happy.

In the middle of arranging her wedding, she had kept herself busy by applying for jobs at places such as Harrods and various offices. She was well qualified and highly intelligent but nothing came her way that suited her.

Anni was offered one job in London but, by now, she was too busy planning her wedding so could not commit to it at that point in her life. Shrien wanted her to do charity work instead and Anni knew she would get work when she wanted after the wedding. She was adored by all who knew her, after all. When she left Stockholm for Luton then later for London, she wrote each and every one of her close colleagues an email thanking them and telling how she would miss them.

She had also brought so much happiness into our lives, it was time she was fulfilled too.

However, there were still rumblings of discontent about her

fiancé among the family.

Anni herself was giving off mixed messages but she had set her heart on marrying Shrien and nobody wanted to stand in her way.

She still worried that he was trying to control her – criticising her dress sense, obsessing about cleanliness. She found it all a bit difficult at times but she knew that nothing was ever perfect.

However in another email to Anish she wrote: "I really love him so much. He is so right for me."

I heard from family members that Anni was working on changing Shrien's appearance, particularly his hairstyle and his clothing, which showed me how interested she was in him and how she wanted to bring out the best of him.

After all, this was a young lady who designed her own clothes and put so much care and attention into looking smart. She only allowed me to wear presentable and stylish shirts which she bought for me. People regularly commented on how handsome I looked in them, which made me proud.

Anni confirmed the changes she was making in another email to Anish: "He makes me so happy. He has even fixed his hair for my sake!"

To Ami she sent a Facebook message which said: "There are many things in life that catch your eye, but only a few that catch your heart."

But she gave hints of a confused heart and mind when she sent another email to Anish which said: "Me and Shrien are together now and it feels right. He is not the world's most handsome guy but definitely the world's most greatest."

I had only met Shrien twice and I had always seen an

extremely presentable young man. He had always been respectful to me as well as to his parents. He and Anni had come a long way since their first dates more than a year earlier when they went to see the musical The Lion King and had dinner at Asia de Cuba in London's West End.

Now they had decided to have a Hindu wedding in India, which would then be followed at some point by a register office ceremony to make it official in the UK. It would be easier for Anni, and everyone else, to purchase Indian clothes and jewellery for the wedding in Mumbai.

Shrien had to return to attend to his family care home business in Bristol and left Anni in Mumbai to organise the wedding, which was to be an elaborate affair held over the course of three days. Of course I worried about her being there alone but a distant relative, who was of a similar age to Anni, supported her and accompanied her on her shopping trips. I was pleased she had a companion to share those three months she would remain in India.

Ever the loving niece, Anni travelled back to Mariestad to surprise Ashok at his 50th birthday on August 14, 2010. It was a wonderful party with over 400 guests and Anni looked fantastic. She was wearing a new blue net sari with red print that she had purchased in India. The blouse, which was made of silk, had been designed by Anni herself. She truly looked like a goddess. She had even taken the time to purchase Sneha's sari and designed her blouse too. Everybody was so happy to see her.

Like any proud uncle, Ashok was very touched that Anni had made the effort to come home for such a landmark event, but we were disappointed that Shrien said he was too busy to attend the party. I'm sure Anni was too.

Anni soon flew back to Mumbai and got to work on planning every detail. Whenever we spoke she sounded so happy. Excited. But she was also a little stressed out over everything that needed to be done.

She sent an email to her brother which revealed how hard the whole thing was on her, having to take care of all the wedding arrangements single handed.

She wrote several emails to Anish, Ami and her cousins, keeping them updated on what she was arranging. In one particular email to Anish she wrote: "I am really happy today. But I am so stressed sometimes. Today, I haven't even had time to eat."

Nilam and I decided to fly to Mumbai to check on her, offer our help and see how things were going. I also wanted to see for myself who she had been doing business with.

I needn't have worried. Anni seemed very comfortable and was evidently enjoying the tasks she had set herself. She had already been in touch with wedding planners, caterers, hotel managers and the people who make the mandap, the stage especially constructed for the priest to marry the bride and groom who walk around a sacred fire four times to seal the ceremony.

I was very impressed with the way Anni had got on with things, organised so much and seemed to be enjoying every minute. She had grown as a person and had become so responsible and self confident. She had this way of talking to people which helped get things exactly the way she wanted. It was amazing to see this change in her. I felt so proud and honoured to have a daughter like her.

Anni introduced me to one particular wedding planner. I felt he was asking a lot, around 600,000 rupees (approximately £60,000), to take over but I didn't voice that.

I didn't need to. Anni said: "Papa, I'll do it." She felt the asking price was far too high and, as she had the time and knew exactly what she wanted, she would do her own wedding planning.

So she organised everything on her own. The photographer, the caterer, the designers, the transport, the hotel, the mandap, the lighting people. Everything. She did it with such style, too. She had always had an eye for these things. She and Sneha had this saying: "It can't be okay, it has be WOW" and Anni truly knew how to "wow" people.

Weeks before the wedding we were very surprised that Anni had done most things on her own. I took my hat off to her that she managed it all in just three months. That was amazing. She built up contacts with the shopkeepers and businessmen, who began calling her their daughter too. She bought matching clothes for everyone, for Nilam and me, my brother, Ami, her husband Henning, their children and Sneha.

Each ceremony was to be different. Every minute detail was being taken care of. I had put no limit on the wedding budget and I never worried about the outlay.

Anni had pursued her wedding plans with such precise detail and with the zest of a young woman excited about the biggest day of her life. She had left nothing at all to chance, right from who was going to be seated where, to the clothes the waiters should wear when serving cocktails.

But the weather was being a problem. It rained regularly

and on one occasion, when we returned to our hired flat in Vile Parle it had rained so much that it was impossible for our rickshaw to take us to the doorstep of the flat.

The water was up to our knees and Anni and I waded through it after a tiring shopping day. I was exhausted, but spurred on by Anni's enthusiasm. We spent many hours and days visiting different shops and all the shopkeepers seemed to know her. She had made so many contacts.

My wife and I returned to Sweden after a fortnight with Anni and were encouraged by her happy demeanour.

We flew back to Mumbai in mid October, about three weeks before the wedding. Shrien's father Prakash had called me a few days before our flight to say his family would keep the accounts as they had good contacts in India and I shouldn't worry about money. He said he needed me to pay him some of the money immediately. I told him I had arranged to transfer money from Sweden and I would pay him without any problems when I reached India. He also sent me an email.

I landed in Mumbai at 6am and we went straight to our rented flat. As soon as the banks opened I was there, withdrawing the amount from my account and putting it in a rucksack.

But Anni rang, distressed. Shrien was in the Breach Candy Hospital in Mumbai and seriously ill. She quite rightly asked us to visit him before we went to deliver the money to the Dewani family.

I felt uncomfortable carrying so much money around Mumbai on my back as I worried that I might leave it somewhere, such as in a taxi, or I could even be robbed.

I agreed that it would be best if we visited our future son-in-law first as that would be respectful and, besides, we were concerned for him. I had no idea what he was being treated for. But at one stage his health was so poor we thought the wedding wouldn't be able to take place and would have to be cancelled.

He obviously didn't like visitors seeing him like that and Anni asked us not to stay too long. We respected his need for privacy and left after a short visit.

After that we went straight by taxi to meet Shrien's brother Preyen at their hotel. I gave the rucksack to him and we joined him for lunch. I was relieved not to be carrying the money around anymore. Preyen didn't count it and I took that as a mark of trust.

I didn't think any more about the money. It was my daughter's wedding and it was my duty to give it to the Dewanis, as I had agreed with Prakash. I later found out that some of the money was to meet the cost of a priest and his wife from the UK who had been invited by the Dewani family. I took exception to that but it was too late to object. We would have got a local priest for a tenth of the cost but I let it go. It wasn't worth having an argument over.

Anni had asked me to bring some chocolates from home. While she was in Mumbai she had read about guests enjoying them at the wedding of Princess Victoria of Sweden that July.

I took 300 packets and 60kgs of sweets at her request. She wanted each guest to have a welcome basket in their hotel room stuffed with the chocolates and sweets, plus mineral water, Bombay mix and other treats. The pretty baskets were decorated by her with colourful netting and flowers.

Anni had bought the baskets from a Mumbai suitcase

manufacturer and convinced these people to remove their company logo and insert "SA" to represent Shrien's initial and her own.

These business people told me my daughter was "remarkable" and they reduced their charges because they became so fond of her. Anni even communicated in Hindi having picked it up so quickly after just three months there.

Shrien's health improved and there was no longer any doubt over the wedding taking place. It was time to forget any problems and enjoy the wedding. Soon guests would be arriving from all over the world, particularly Sweden, the UK, Africa, India and the USA. Finally, the big day was upon us.

It was time to enjoy.

Chapter 13

A conundrum for me

Cape Town, South Africa
December, 2010

The next few days, just like the previous ones, were to be a thorough roller coaster for myself and my family with our emotions and our hearts battered and beaten.

As I prepared to leave South Africa, with the promise from the authorities that the case would be closed with Shrien's quick and impending return and the charges against Mngeni and Qwabe being processed, events were moving rapidly back in Bristol and London.

My son-in-law had been arrested, kept in police cells and driven to London to make his first court appearance.

Some members of my family including Sneha attended the Royal Courts of Justice in London to see him in handcuffs embarking on the long road to justice. At this stage, nobody could predict just how long or short the process might be.

The Senior District Judge Howard Riddle ordered Shrien to spend a second night in custody while his family registered a £250,000 surety. Police told the court the huge bail bond was necessary because Shrien had the means to abscond. His passport would be confiscated.

116

A lawyer for the South Africans told the court that police had uncovered evidence placing Shrien at the centre of the hit on my daughter. The information had come from the hotel worker Mbolombo, who was not being charged for introducing Tongo to the two gunmen after the alleged request from Shrien.

As I left Cape Town there were reports that police had seized CCTV footage of Shrien paying Tongo, although at that stage I wasn't sure what to make of it.

I am a great believer in due process and the fair delivery of justice and was glad to learn that Judge Riddle had commented: "Either Mr Dewani over a period of time plotted the murder of his wife or he is one of the tragic victims of this incident."

That, in a nutshell, was the conundrum for me.

I tried very hard myself not to be judge and jury against Shrien. If I had been asked at the time for my true feelings about him, it would be an understatement to say that they would probably have been less than lukewarm. That would have been for the manner he cold-shouldered my daughter.

However, some of my family could not hold back or keep their feelings and views to themselves. Ami was quoted on the front page of The Times newspaper: "If he is guilty, then what he has done is unforgivable. You can't just kill somebody. It is scary. What the hell was he thinking?"

Ami spoke for all the family when she described how difficult life was going to be without Anni.

"It is terrible enough to lose a sister, but it is even more terrible to lose a sister in such a way.

"We were at her wedding only two weeks ago. It is such a

struggle. But the saddest part in all of this is that it doesn't matter what happens to Shrien, to the driver or to whoever killed her. I will never get my sister back."

Paying tribute to dear Anni, she added: "Anni was a very talkative, happy person. She was always smiling. Whoever she met, she would bring joy into that person's life."

At the same time there were some not so kind words for Shrien from South Africa's National Police Commissioner, General Bheki Cele, who described Shrien as a "monkey."

This was a serious, harrowing time for all concerned, so people should not have been making cretinous remarks so freely.

Cele appeared to be trying to protect his country when he said: "One monkey came from London to kill his wife here. He thought we South Africans were stupid. Don't kill people here."

I knew these words could be seen as inflammatory and I was quickly on the phone to the prosecutors to register my disquiet.

In the meantime, a photograph of Anni looking relaxed and happy also emerged. It was taken four days before her life was ended, enjoying her honeymoon in the Sabi Sand Game Reserve. It was published in the UK press and just made me smile and miss her even more.

Day after day, new claims, facts and other information emerged in the media.

But in my meetings with the prosecutors and the police in Cape Town, never once had there been a hint of the motive for Shrien's alleged involvement. The driver Tongo and the other two hitmen had seemingly been motivated by the opportunity to rob two unsuspecting tourists on their honeymoon.

Yet Shrien stood accused. I could not figure out in my head why, if the claims were true, would he do this? Why? He had money, looks, charm, an education, a loving family and now a beautiful young woman who had promised to spend the rest of her life with him. They would have children, build a family home and be the bright shining couple everybody adored.

Why would he, as it was claimed, get involved with such a plot to stage a robbery and murder Anni?

I was all for the police continuing with their investigation and the courts ultimately deciding innocence or guilt, but I could not fathom why Shrien would do this and why the police accepted Tongo's accusation against Shrien so easily.

Then we discovered that Shrien had been keeping something from us, perhaps even from Anni. This revelation made us question how much we really knew about him.

On Friday December 10, 2010, a headline appeared in one of the UK tabloids which read: "I'm not gay." It purported to be a denial from Shrien as the police investigated rumours.

It appeared Shrien had been asked directly if he was gay and he had shaken his head and said: "One of the big talks we had on honeymoon was about starting a family."

It would have been in very poor taste to ask anybody about their sexuality and I have no problems at all with people who are gay or lesbian. But the headline stuck with me. Why even ask it in the first place? What did this have to do with anything?

We'd heard Shrien didn't want to sleep with Anni at first – he kept pushing her away, saying he did not believe in sex before marriage. He'd also had that mysterious fertility problem which caused them to break up and reunite once he said he had been successfully treated.

Could it have actually been a ploy to hide his true sexuality? We had met him only twice and he had rejected invitations to attend family events. I wondered now if he had been anxious we might suspect him of hiding something.

Then there was the episode before the wedding when he was admitted to hospital with his illness never fully being explained. We knew only that he may have had food poisoning.

Was he clever enough to keep his distance in case we realised he was a homosexual in the time leading up to the wedding? The questions started spinning in my head and I didn't really know what to believe. The whole scenario was just strange.

So if he was gay, how could I have missed it? To be fair, it was the last thing any father would suspect if a man asks to marry his daughter after romancing her in the way he did.

Anni would certainly not have married him, if he was indeed into men. She was a woman who loved children and I saw this every time she was with her niece and nephew. She wanted a family. She wanted to be loved back, with her looks, intelligence and warm heart, she could have her pick of men. So there was no way she was going to marry a man who was also into men. No way at all. No way.

But the thought had been planted and I could not get it out of my mind. It was the talk of my whole family, whether Anni and the rest of us had been hoodwinked. It was such a startling headline but I could not get any confirmation from the police or the prosecutors and I believed they had to keep their cards close to their chest while they built the case against Shrien.

The gay claim was put by the media to the Dewani spokesman Max Clifford and he sneered: "Every day there is a different rumour and just about all of them are as full of nonsense as this one."

But whenever I checked the internet there appeared to be references to Shrien being gay and claims that his sexuality had been an "open" secret.

It certainly hadn't been that open, or it would have been circulating within my family. Everybody I asked about whether they had any information or previous suspicions returned negative responses. Nobody had a clue how this information came to be doing the rounds and, by now, the Dewani family and the Hindochas were on non-speaking terms.

I'd presumed that would happen. I had generally got along with Prakash, who was the head of the Dewani family. But now with his son under arrest for conspiring to murder my daughter, there wasn't really that much to say between us. He would be hoping his son would be cleared while I was just hoping for the whole truth about what happened.

All ties between us were duly cut once Shrien had been detained and the spotlight had fallen on him and his behaviour on the night of Anni's murder.

Shrien was eventually granted his freedom on bail after two nights in custody.

In South Africa, things were moving incredibly fast with regards to the investigation and police were releasing new information by the minute.

CCTV film, handed to the police, showed Shrien meeting Tongo several times at the Cape Grace Hotel. In some of the footage, which I saw along with millions of others around the world on the news, you could actually see me sitting in the hotel as Shrien left my side and went to meet and pay Tongo. It was taken three days after the hijacking.

It was a curious piece of film and I wondered how my son-in-law could bring himself to meet with Tongo that day without me and then apparently hand over a bag to him.

What was actually in that bag bothered me greatly and I was mystified about why it was important at that time – so important that he left a room where his wife's grieving father was sitting.

Most would agree that I had a vested interest in speaking to Tongo at that moment, mere days after my daughter's death, and possibly even offering him my sympathy for what he had gone through too. It would have been very appropriate for me to have questioned him about Anni and what happened that night. He had been there. I hadn't and I needed to know what had happened.

I had been given only bits of the story upon my arrival in Cape Town that very first time and Tongo would, at the very least, have been able to fill in some gaps with his perspective on events.

At that point I was still in shock and I would clutch at every scrap of information, even though they were very thin on the ground, about Anni's last few hours. If I had been given the opportunity to talk with him, I would have asked him a lot of questions about his version of what had happened that night. But for Shrien to give him the money he owed him for his taxi services, if that was what it was for, so soon after his wife had died, should have ranked lower in importance. I felt angry watching this footage on the news.

I was not to know then that the police believed there were different reasons why the taxi driver made that early visit to the Cape Grace.

Chapter 14

The bride looked 'WOW!'

Mumbai, India
October, 2010

It was typical of the good fortune that had followed Anni for most of her life.

The three days that would see her marriage to Shrien sealed had arrived. It had stopped raining and the sun came out as if it was a special blessing for the bride. We were all delighted.

It was still very sticky, hot and humid. Mumbai was a good place to sweat off the pounds whenever you ventured outside. The turn in the weather seemed to help lift the mood among most of the wedding party, although something appeared to be bothering Anni. Her natural exuberance seemed to be stifled. I could see by her eyes that she was troubled.

I could sense it when I looked at her but, once again, I put it down to the stress and tension of ensuring everything went to plan, ran smoothly and, most importantly, on time.

There is a saying in my motherland that everything is scheduled and reliant on "Indian timing." This had commonly been known to involve people shaking their heads in agreement that orders will be carried out to your requirements, only for the work to be completed when it suits everybody but yourself.

To be fair, India has moved on a great deal in my lifetime and is undoubtedly now a superpower, with both the UK and the US vying for prime position as its partner in international trade as well as political affinity.

However we as Swedes and Britons were all too well aware that some people might try to exploit our foreign bank balances and fail to deliver in return. It meant Anni having to be extra vigilant that everything she'd ordered and agreed to pay for wasn't overpriced and would also surface on time.

I was glad that Sneha was to be by her side throughout the ceremonies. Sneha was like a sister to Anni, even though she was her cousin. They shared everything, all their secrets, and spent each available hour together.

It was Sneha who had secretly helped Shrien organise the engagement trip to Paris. She gave Anni's passport to Shrien and went with him to Selfridges in London, where she helped pick out the black silk size six Karen Millen dress, and size three Christian Dior shoes that were presented to her in Paris before the £25,000 diamond engagement ring. Shrien had joked that he was going to turn an "ugly duckling into a swan."

Later Sneha told me it was the first occasion in her life that she had kept anything from Anni. They had a pact to always tell each other all their secrets. Their agreement was never broken until Shrien took Anni to Paris that day from an Oxford airstrip by private jet. When my daughter landed in France she asked airport ground staff which language they spoke before she realised which country she was in!

Anni adored the pink Laurent-Perrier Champagne, and her

much-loved salt and vinegar crisps that Shrien organised to be on the plane. The red roses he presented to her would have melted her heart.

Sneha was with Anni whenever she needed her. In Mumbai, Anni bought Sneha a blue net sari by the top Indian fashion designer Ritu Kumar to wear at the wedding and joked with her that Sneha would look prettier than her. She told Sneha that Ritu had designed a sari for a former Miss World and that Sneha would look even better.

Anni told her: "I am going to look uglier than you on my day. You will be more beautiful."

Sneha, being the loving friend that she was, offered to swap saris with Anni. But my daughter told her she was only kidding.

Anni and Sneha were like the proverbial two peas in a pod. They went everywhere together in Mumbai in the days leading up to the wedding. In effect, Sneha was also acting as the wedding planner. She kept an A4 diary in which she and Anni inserted the three-day wedding schedule. After each event or task, Sneha would tick it off as completed.

When Anni went to buy her wedding sari she tried on outfit after outfit much to the bemusement of the shop staff. She then made the staff take pictures of her on her BlackBerry before emailing them straight to Sneha, who couldn't be there, for comments. As the wedding designs are exclusive to the store they usually do not allow anyone to take pictures of them, but in this case they couldn't say no to Anni.

The two young women giggled their way around Mumbai, looking at jewellery, saris, shoes and gifts for family members. It was an absolute picture of happiness. Sneha just went along with it when Anni chose her outfits as she trusted her to know her taste and style. It always seemed to work out.

In return, Sneha was given the right to choose Anni's clothes for her honeymoon, although nothing had been decided as to where the newlyweds would head at that stage.

Sneha and Anni had grown up together, having been born a year apart, and here they were planning the next stage of Anni's life with Shrien.

I regard Sneha as my daughter, as are all my nieces, and all my nephews are like my sons. My love for them is beyond measure. My family thrives on its closeness and our respect for each other. Each has excelled in their chosen career paths and not one has taken a penny from the state. They have all completed their education and headed off on their own paths in life – from disc-jockey to engineering and banking. They are the shining jewels of the Hindocha family and its future.

Anni was a sight to behold throughout the three days of official wedding functions and celebrations. The festivities began on the afternoon of October 28 with the chundari ceremony, which is one of the events that precede the wedding. It took place on the rooftop of the hotel. The 350 guests who attended were first given a delicious vegetarian Indian buffet lunch, served in the grounds of the hotel.

Anni had instructed waiting staff to help escort the elderly and less able guests up the steep flights of stairs to their seats, which was typical of her thoughtful nature. Other waiters, wearing black waistcoats and white gloves, stood at the entrance with trays of ice cold soft drinks.

Nilam, Sneha and I stood at the entrance to greet the Dewanis and their guests as they arrived. They walked in with a musician banging the dhol drum. Nilam gave each visitor a red rose and boxes of sweets. Sneha garlanded the groom with a necklace of red roses. Then the girls from Anni's side celebrated the arrival of the groom by dancing to the dhol. This is a very common gesture at Indian weddings which lifted the joyous mood even further.

After Shrien had sat down and carried out some obligatory religious exchanges with the priest, Anni walked in along the red carpet looking simply… well… Wow! There were no other words to describe such a moment. I felt my eyes watering with pride.

Sneha and Anni had a choice phrase when something was beyond amazing and that word was "Wow." I have had it instilled in my vocabulary and have used it myself many times after hearing the two young woman repeat it so often. That day, Anni looked completely: "Wow!"

Shrien's family gave Anni a green sari, which is one of the traditions performed at the chundari that the groom's family follow. She draped it over her pink outfit as she stood on the stage with Shrien, who was dressed in a gold tunic and, I have to say, they looked a very handsome couple indeed.

The Dewanis and their friends also brought an array of gifts, mostly saris and bangles, which is another expected custom. Anni gracefully accepted the gifts, with Ami at her side.

As the temperature was uncomfortably hot, the waiters were instructed to keep handing out cold towels to guests for their comfort.

As the guests left, my two sister-in-laws gave the guests gifts from the Hindocha family of boxes of dandiya. These are used in the Gujarati garba folk dance when families come together and pace around, clashing the pieces of wood together. They were ordered by Anni and, once again, she showed her artistic flair by finding ones with small lights in them, so they lit up when banged together during garba.

Later I learned that Anni had asked Sneha: "Do I look pretty?" My daughter had returned to her room to relax for the day after the chundari ceremony and Sneha had questioned her as to why she would even need to ask such a thing. Anni replied that Shrien had told her: "Your sari doesn't look very proper." Sneha had consoled her, telling her she looked amazing. Shrien was so wide of the mark, she assured her.

Anni also told her confidante Sneha that she and her fiancé had decided to "act for the rest of the wedding." Sneha was shocked. She felt under extreme pressure and unsure what to say in reply. With so many people already there and with the cost, preparation and organisation, she decided to encourage Anni to go through with the rest of the ceremonies, telling her that she could always leave him if it didn't get better and seek a divorce. She told Anni she just wanted her to be happy.

I know Sneha has worried ever since that she said the wrong thing but, at the end of the day, it was Anni's decision alone to go through with the wedding. Sneha had only said what any one of us would have said. Anni was constantly changing her mind and we all put it down to routine wedding tension.

Anni had also, a few days earlier, begged Sneha to "take me away from all of this" but Sneha believed it was just nerves. Stress. Just like we all did. Sneha did ask Anni what she would advise, if the roles were reversed. Anni had responded by saying she would tell Sneha to get married and seek a divorce if it couldn't work out.

Anni also confided that she believed Shrien had been "lying" about his fertility problems. Sneha had asked her how she could be so sure and Anni had replied: "Trust me, I know." Sneha took this to mean that Shrien had been refusing to sleep with Anni and she had made up her mind that, for whatever reason, he was using his supposed testosterone problem as an excuse to avoid having sex with her.

They'd mostly had separate beds when they were together from the earliest point in their relationship.

Sneha did come and talk to Nilam and me about this very late one night. But I dismissed Anni's fears and told Sneha to reassure her that Shrien was probably suffering problems due to his illness and the tension of getting married.

I was convinced this would all blow over, once the marriage had been finalised and the young couple had stopped being the centre of attention and were given time alone together. The gulf between the bride and groom would surely disappear once they were married, I hoped.

Sneha, who never lied or kept secrets from Anni, apart from the Paris engagement surprise, told Anni she had been to see me and her mother and woken us up during the middle of the night. Anni was keen to know what I had said, which shows she must have been seeking an opinion on her dilemma from somebody she loved and trusted.

Sneha had found it embarrassing to talk about such a subject with me, but there was no need, as she was only motivated by love and her care for Anni. I will always treasure

Sneha for what she did for Anni.

But what a terrible situation Anni was in.

There had been problems in the year leading up to this day, but as I looked at them I could only see two young people about to embark on the most important journey of their lives in marriage.

Shrien pushing Anni away, saying nasty things and trying to control her were all buried at the back of my mind. These three days were to be filled with celebration as my youngest daughter married her prince. There were only smiles on the faces around me.

A multitude of mendhi artists arrived in the afternoon to decorate the arms of the bride, the ladies in Anni's entourage and other guests with henna and turmeric paste.

The importance of the mendhi depends on whom you speak to and what you read and believe. But folklore has it that the darker the colour of the mendhi, the more the bride's husband will love her.

Some say the bride should not be expected to work in her marital house until her mendhi has faded away. Anni had applied her mendhi the night before and ordered a stronger tone while the guests had a paler turmeric strength which would fade after a couple of days.

As evening fell, the mendhi ceremony began. The entrance was opened by Anni's cousin-sisters, as they called themselves, Sneha, Mishalli, Nishma and Nira who walked in holding candles. The four ladies wore green skirts and purple blouses, which had been chosen and bought by Anni herself. She had taken everyones measurements so that her designer could ensure each outfit was a perfect fit.

Anni walked behind her cousins accompanied by Shrien. She wore a green and red outfit and a huge gold necklace with matching earrings, her arms draped in bangles. She looked absolutely stunning. She was wearing the mendhi outfit she had bought in India with myself and Nilam. I later learnt that she hadn't liked the original blouse, so she had designed a whole new one. Now it looked amazing.

Anni could easily have been a Bollywood star as she walked in, the video cameraman trailing her as we all applauded this vision of beauty, Shrien at her side.

Anni, the wedding planner and bride, had arranged a red carpet for guests to walk along. A red silk drape had been hung over the entrance covered in pink and white flowers. Column after column was decorated in blossoms.

Another entrance was bedecked in red and white primroses with a silk curtain draped on two pillars beneath them. Anni had arranged for them to be floodlit and they looked very colourful and decorative. At the foot of the pillars were two large silver bowls filled with water and floating flowers.

She had chosen full size statues of Radha and Krishna, Hindu god and goddess, to be placed in front of the stage. The statues had orange flower garlands placed over them. Anni wanted an Arabic theme to the decorations and the banqueting hall had been filled with Bedouin-style tents covered in flowers and silk drapes with red velvet chaises inside them. I could not believe the transformation of this room.

She and Shrien walked through the well-wishers' applause and on to the stage, where they sat on chairs covered in gold silk. They also lit a diya oil lamp. The flame is extremely sacred and important at Hindu weddings.

Anni had left no detail to chance and once again I admired her vision in creating this spectacle.

We were witnessing three months of Anni's creativity. It was her big day and she clearly wanted it to be memorable for her as well as every guest who attended. In the background, women sang traditional songs wishing the bride a prosperous marital life and clapped along as the pair smiled and hugged guests.

It was a formal Hindu marriage ritual but the affection in the room, and the number of young people, helped keep everyone at ease.

Hindu weddings and their rituals date back centuries but there is always a sense of fun and jocularity surrounding the Vedic requirements. One of the humorous developments over the years has been for the bride to have her groom's name or initials written in henna and hidden on her arm so he has to try to seek it out.

In this case Anni had the henna artist inscribe Shrien's name over the crossing of her right thumb and on to her palm next to a drawing of a Maharaja and his Maharani. I never found out if he managed to see it and whether he saw the funny side of it.

The ever-faithful Sneha gave a wonderful speech with the help of a PowerPoint presentation, which was a funny and innovative idea. She started by introducing herself and said: "To me, she is not just my cousin, she is my best friend and my sister. Someone I can confide in and someone who has always been there for me since I was born."

She then showed her first graphic which had these five bullet points and was entitled "Anni's best qualities."

* Caring.
* Thinks about others before herself.
* Generous.
* Honest.
* Always looks for the silver lining.

Then the party burst into laughter when Sneha showed her second image which had the title "Anni's bad qualities". There was a picture of a kitchen with a No Entry sign across it and the single bullet point:

* Her skills in the kitchen.

Sneha went on to tell the audience: "When we were younger, Anni and I were in her kitchen making some pasta. Something was wrong with the saucepan as it got really hot and we didn't know what to do with it, so we put it on the plastic floor (another one of Anni's crazy ideas). The floor got a big burn mark and Anni suggested that we should cover it up with the carpet. Needless to say, as soon as Aunty Nilam came home, Anni confessed everything, but this time she was too scared to tell Vinod.

"Luckily for you, Shrien, Anni has had a lot of practice in her cooking skills since then. When we first moved to the UK, Anni was a "stay at home wife" whilst I used to go to work. Every day when I got home she had already prepared the food for me as she knew that I would be hungry after a long day at work.

"Anni, please move back home – I miss my hot food when I come home."

There was raucous laughter at The Sneha Show and both bride and groom were in hysterics. Then Sneha and Anish acted out the couple's characters with jokes about their first date, their clothes and dining habits.

It was a splendid way to finish off the evening.

Chapter 15

Bitterness between the two families

Mariestad, Sweden
December, 2010

The South Africans duly applied for, and received, the extradition permit they needed, enabling the UK courts to ensure Shrien boarded a plane back to Cape Town to face questioning and trial for murdering Anni.

The National Prosecuting Authority presented the papers to its Department of Justice. A spokesman for the latter organisation said Shrien would be returned to South Africa "very soon."

Officially the South Africans had 45 days to present the extradition order to the British Home Office for rubber stamping.

I'd learnt there was an agreement in place for transporting suspects between the two countries but I had no idea how long it would take. By now Shrien's family had accused the South Africans of manufacturing the case against him to protect its booming tourist industry.

They claimed the evidence was "flimsy and flawed." There was also the first suggestion that Shrien would not, after all, be a willing witness or be volunteering himself to the South

African authorities. Christmas was approaching and his lawyers were working hard to stop his extradition.

I was already a little sick of talking to officials about the case. I was missing Anni so very badly and seeing her mother in such anguish day after day was very difficult.

A full night's sleep become rare, almost impossible. We would wake in the early hours and talk about our daughter. There were still so many questions and the biggest was why. Why Anni? Why our family? Why did those evil people shoot her when she was so defenceless and the robbery had already taken place?

They could have just released her. They could have pushed her out of the vehicle too. They had a gun, a loaded gun, and she was a girl who could not fight back. There was no need to shoot her and kill her. It was an act of enormous cowardice and evil.

Nilam and I went over it for hours and hours on so many nights, whether Anni would have stood any chance at all of escaping with her life. With Shrien gone, she would have been alone. I wondered if she would have realised Shrien was no longer in the taxi because one of the police officers in Cape Town told me the killers had admitted she said: "Don't shoot us." That was Anni – worried not only about herself but her husband too, and when she said "us" I believed she must have thought her husband was still by her side.

Shrien's impending appointment with the law officers was not our biggest concern, although the delay was frustrating as I knew neither Nilam nor I could properly mourn Anni until we knew the full story.

Some so-called "facts" were clearly wrong but very painful

for us to read. A paramedic who went to the scene submitted a report to the investigation team and it somehow found its way into the hands of journalists in the British media. The paramedic had detailed Anni's wounds and reported that she had two or three stab wounds to her back in addition to the bullet wound.

I was assured this claim was unfounded but it still caused me great anxiety and was an example of the extra difficulties arising out of the fact that this was an international issue. Anni was a young woman from a Swedish family who was murdered in South Africa and her accused husband was British with a case against him being pursued in the country where the crime was committed. The legal action necessary to take Shrien to South Africa was being focused in the UK courts, while we were observing developments in both countries from our home in Mariestad.

Some friends of my daughter wrote an open letter, which was partly published in some of the media, in which they urged Shrien to go back to Cape Town and leave the case to the police and courts. Apparently, his relatives had dispatched emails to other family members and friends to start a media campaign to help clear his name.

It was said to be a response from remarks by Max Clifford claiming that Shrien was carrying a Barbie doll to remind him of Anni. I did not like how Clifford was briefed on my daughter's childhood love for her Barbie dolls. And I was unhappy that Anni's early years were being used in a publicity campaign to ensure Shrien was seen in the public eye as a heartbroken husband yearning for his bride.

He hadn't shown that affection for her in front of us after

she had passed away. He'd been guilty of the most insulting behaviour as we stood around her body in the hour before her cremation.

Journalists could not be allowed to rely solely on Clifford for information. Ashok stepped up to become my family's spokesman. By now the media and public interest was very high and Ashok is a brave man who is not fazed by new challenges. He knew nothing about the tabloid world or how television worked but he was always engaging and friendly to the media and they trusted him when they asked for comments. I worried that he had shelved his own grief at losing his niece to best approach the heavy media pressure put on us.

Our wish, which we decided very early on was the right thing, was that it was up to the courts to hear Shrien's case. Until that was over we would not be commenting on whether he was involved in Anni's murder or not.

That would not have been fair on Shrien or the investigating team until we knew more about what happened on that terrible night.

But I did make one offhand remark which was to be printed and repeated many times and which I would come to regret.

I was speaking with the intention of making Shrien's path back to Cape Town both easier and quicker when I said I would put my arm around his shoulder and travel back with him to South Africa if he wanted me to. I would do the same when we came home if he was cleared.

I came to realise the press was going to be a key part in the whole process of seeing Shrien returned to Cape Town. The media world was a giant which none of my family understood. I admired Ashok for the way he got on with its representatives.

Stories about Anni, the investigation, Shrien, South African violence and the extradition order were appearing from all corners and their revelations were often a mystery to us.

But Ashok hit on something so potent very early on when he realised Anni was being treated like the least important person and subject in the whole episode. It felt like she was being forgotten.

We agreed that it was vital to keep talking about an innocent woman who had lost her life on her honeymoon and let everything else take care of itself. Anni and her family were not the first thing on the minds of the South African officers when they woke in the morning and certainly not on the minds of Max Clifford or Shrien's family.

My daughter, the real victim in all this, had to stay at the centre of whatever ensued. Ashok came to hear from reporters that her beauty meant it was easy for her photograph to make the pages of the newspapers. As her father, I was heartened that it was being universally accepted she was a pretty young woman, and perhaps the large media attention would contribute positively to the case.

Though, I truly did not understand what the coverage really meant or how it worked, but if Max Clifford was going to be speaking up on behalf of Shrien, then it was our job as a family to keep talking about Anni.

We were always going to be careful not to interfere in the legal process but we could talk about Anni as much as we wanted because she was the victim.

The kiss-and-tell publicist hired by Shrien gave out some

video footage of Anni dancing with her new husband at the wedding. Looking at the film, any independent observer would have seen a good-looking young couple, arm in arm, gazing into each other's eyes and smiling as they twirled around having been newly married.

It was broadcast on the television in the UK and South Africa and was designed to show the love the couple had for each other when they married. I, of course, had been told that Anni had said they were just "acting", in order to avoid conflict during the ceremony.

But whatever spin Clifford put on it, the South Africans were working hard on the case and as the new year began we learned through newspaper reports that police in Cape Town had apprehended another man who had admitted being involved in Anni's murder.

This was the hotel worker, Monde Mbolombo. He had given police a statement that he had been contacted by Tongo and he put the taxi driver in contact with Qwabe and Mngeni.

It was a surprising new development but we stuck rigidly to our plan. I told reporters that Shrien had nothing to be afraid of if he hadn't been involved in murdering Anni and that he should still go back to South Africa and identify her killers. He had said that he would not be able to recognise the killers, I found this strange as I know that I would never forget the face of someone who had killed my wife and put a gun to my head.

One of Shrien's cousins, Akta Raja, and a lawyer named Andrew Jackson wrote an article in the Sunday Telegraph in which they questioned whether the judge in Cape Town would give him a fair trial because he had apparently been accused of misconduct in the past.

I thought this was a very tricky path for Shrien and his public relation advisers to follow and made no comment on the matter at all. Surely guilt or innocence should be decided by a judge in a court of law and not by a cousin writing in a newspaper.

Not to be outdone, Ashok released one of the text messages Anni had sent home from South Africa in which she described crying as being her new hobby. I wasn't savvy enough to understand what was going on but I felt maybe Ashok believed if videos had been circulated of Anni and Shrien dancing and looking so happy, then perhaps some solid material which showed the other side of the Anni and Shrien wedding story should also be shown.

My youngest brother was also showing signs of frustration and told another reporter that Shrien had not done enough to protect Anni when he left the taxi and left her alone and scared.

The bitterness between the families was beginning to spill out. There was concern among my family about a school the Dewanis were proposing to build in India using funds from a charity set up in Anni's name. We had not been consulted at all and were furious when we read Shrien's family had said we had supported the idea.

We had hoped to find some solace in the quiet calm of Sweden, but with the murder making headlines around the world, there was to be no peace. Naturally, I wanted to be kept abreast of events in South Africa and in the UK regarding the extradition. But Anni's photograph appearing in the newspapers and on our TV screens was almost a daily occurrence.

A woman who had befriended Anni on her honeymoon safari at Chitwa Chitwa Game Lodge came forward to say Shrien had hardly touched or kissed his wife during their time together. Anni had been excited about a girls' night out with her and her friend later and had agreed to meet them in Cape Town on the weekend she was killed.

The woman, who was younger than Anni, said they had swapped numbers and she had called Shrien when she found out about Anni's murder.

He told her: "It's been a disaster from start to finish."

I am sure that announcement was a hasty response to a call from a woman who was almost a stranger. But his remark to her was one of the biggest understatements in the whole sorry relationship.

Chapter 16

Goodbye

Mumbai, India
October 29, 2010

The Chundari and Mendhi ceremonies had gone well and today – October 29 – was the day of Anni's marriage. The sun was beginning to set on the banks of Lake Powai as 350 well-wishers gathered at the Renaissance Hotel. Anni had brought her own sunshine.

It was a big and grand wedding and we had booked hotel rooms for all of our guests. Everyone from Sweden and the UK were staying at the same place and had done so since the ceremonies started the day before.

Anni was my second and last daughter. I wanted to give her the dream wedding she had hoped for. After all, one of Anni's smiles was worth twice any amount. I did not put any limit to how much she could spend as I wanted her big day to be perfect.

As a result, no expense had been spared from the flowers to the cocktails, from the top-quality food served to guests to the red carpet laid out for the bride and groom. This wedding was going to be incredible. It should be the proudest day in any young woman's life as well as her parents.

But my concerns about the couple resurfaced on the morning when we staged the pre-wedding mandvo ceremony, when prayers are held to invite Lord Ganesh to give his blessing for the wedding later.

The Mandvo ceremony is performed by the respective families alone. All those from the bride's side attend the bride's Mandvo and all the groom's side attend the groom's Mandvo. The same priest is used in both ceremonies so they have to take place one after another.

Anni's Mandvo was amazing. When she arrived in her orange and green sari once again she looked stunning, glowing like only a bride can. The ceremony was held outside under a shelter from the sun. Anni came walking down the stone path with the wind in her hair and she looked like a model. The atmosphere was really relaxed as it was just our family and Anni's friends. Everyone had the chance to follow and be a part of the ceremony. Anni seemed really relaxed. She was enjoying herself, joking with the priest and appeared comfortable with her surroundings.

I have been a Hindu for all of my 65 years but I admit some of the rituals are difficult to comprehend. I swear there are millions of Hindus like me around the world who understand some or most of the aspects of our beautiful religion, but not all.

It is a fascinating and sincere religion full of poetry. One which promotes kindness to all others. But I have never grasped the whole understanding of all our rituals. I simply learn as I go on.

It was, I suppose, called "going with the flow" and we did just that as our guests looked on.

This was the last ceremony before the wedding. Now it was time to get ready for the wedding itself.

I could sense Anni's unease but I was encouraged by the fact that both the Chundari and Mendhi ceremonies had passed off without incident and that she and Shrien were all smiles the previous night.

It was only later I discovered that Anni, with a few hours to go before she was married, had given a dire warning of the seriousness of the situation between her and the man she was about to marry.

Sneha had tended to Anni's hair and make-up before the ceremony. As the cousins prepared, Sneha had asked if things had improved between her and her fiancé.

Anni had responded: "No, I told you we are just acting. It is still the same."

Sneha had told her she hoped things would work out and if they didn't she reminded her that she could seek a divorce. Anni had told her that if the roles had been reversed, she would have advised her to do the same. Sneha appreciated that.

At 3pm Shrien arrived. The groom always arrives before the bride. It wasn't the kind of fanfare that we expected. One of the two elephants that had been hired to greet his arrival began to get fidgety and started darting around in an agitated state as he walked by. At one stage it reared on to its hind legs and its trainer had to struggle to regain control. It scared a few people.

Still, Shrien looked very smart in his gold and sequinned sherwani tunic, turban with peacock feathers and gold shoes with curled up toes. He also wore a diamond brooch on the

turban with a string of pearls hanging to the right side of it
and a sparkly bindi on his forehead. He was accompanied to
the mandap by his brother Preyen, sister Preyal and mother
and father. Both Preyen and his father wore similar gold
coloured tunics and long scarves. The women wore flowing
saris and all looked fantastic.

The scene for the wedding had been a design creation of
Anni's and there was universal agreement that it was one of
the best mandaps ever seen by most guests. I have a friend
who is an events manager from Bangalore and when he saw
it he was astonished. He asked me how a young woman who
was brought up in Europe could have such incredible artistic
talent as well as understanding of the sacred Vedic Hindu
wedding rites. It was, I have to agree, a very spectacular
mandap and Anni had designed it all by herself.

She had assembled a gifted team of designers who had
worked from her drawings to build the stage, which must have
been 30 foot high. It had a dome, which was covered in
flowers and gold silk drapes. Hundreds of lights were built
into the lower rim and the pillars and the whole structure
was floodlit from beneath with pink and yellow beams of
light. There was a red carpet on the stage floor and Indian
ornaments were all around. The seats where Anni and Shrien
were to sit, alongside all four parents and the priest, were
covered in white silk and had golden bows tied across them.

It truly was a fantastic sight and I took a moment to take
it all in, admiring the vast outdoor area, which had similar
ornate seats, and the canopy outer wall with its gold silk lining.

Sneha told me this had been Anni's dream, to have the most
brilliant mandap, and at one stage in the planning she had

thought about re-creating the Taj Mahal on the stage. She had quickly changed her mind after worrying the wedding could turn circus-like if she had attempted copying the famous building.

It is traditional for the bride's wedding dress to be paid for by her mother's brothers. Anni had bought a wedding sari and presented it to a tailor to cut, stitch and modify exactly the way she wanted. Being thoughtful as always, Anni had asked me to pay for it as she said it would be unfair on her uncles. But they insisted on paying the whole amount because they loved her so much. Even the tailor described her as "my sister" and instead of charging 200,000 rupees he asked for 60,000. Anni had made such an impression on him, he loved her like a brother would a sister.

Anni was carried into the wedding area by her uncles Ashok, Vipul, Bharat, and Piyoosh, plus her brother Anish and cousin Nikesh on a gold leafed chair, sitting on a red cushion. They were all wearing sherwanis and looked smarter than I had ever seen them before.

When I caught sight of Anni in her wedding sari my heart melted. She was smiling and looking majestic. Like a princess.

She had expressly asked that I did not see her in her wedding dress until she was to be married, telling me: "Papa, I don't want you to see me in my wedding sari until the moment." It had been worth the wait.

Both Nilam and I smiled broadly and clapped along to the music from the live band as Anni was carried in at shoulder height, the bearers taking great care to ensure they didn't drop her.

There were red and white flowers placed by her side and her

green jewel-encrusted sari sparkled brightly. She had about a dozen bangles on her arm, long earrings and a diamond hanging from her hair on to her forehead.

I knew I was going to get emotional and there was no holding back as I wiped tears from my face. I was so, so proud of Anni.

Anni and Shrien exchanged garlands as they walked on to the mandap and the priest, who had been flown from Britain by the Dewanis, began the ceremony.

Sneha and Ami took turns in sitting alongside Anni. Shrien's siblings took their places next to the groom.

I looked at Anni's feet and there, right next to her, was a framed photograph of her dada, my father. I was extremely proud that she had wanted her late grandfather included in some way, even though he had passed on years earlier. My mother, Ba, was also on the stage and she appreciated the gesture.

Just as the wedding was about to begin, my guests sitting near the mandap were asked to move by Prakash. He wanted to seat his family and friends there. Naturally, we obliged, although I was cross that this had happened as the ceremony began. The Dewanis had no right to demand who sat where.

It was not the best start to proceedings and things quickly got worse. During the mangal phera, when the couple walk around the sacred fire four times to affirm their marriage, the fire went out on the third circle.

The mangal pheras are made around the fire in a clockwise direction representing four goals in life: dharma (religious and moral duties), artha (prosperity), kama (earthly pleasures) and moksha (spiritual salvation and liberation).

To have the flame go out is seen as a sign of very bad luck for the bride and groom and their marriage. Nilam and I looked at each other in panic but said nothing as the flames turned to thick smoke. There was lots of smoke. The priest quickly added more ghee (butter) and tried to relight it but the last phera was done without being lit which left us feeling a little uneasy.

Shrien and Anni took vows to respect and honour each other, to share one another's joy and sorrow, to trust and be loyal to each other, to cultivate knowledge, values, sacrifice and service. They confirmed their vows of purity, love, family duties and spiritual growth and to follow principles of dharma (righteousness) and to nurture an eternal bond of friendship and love.

Both Nilam and I agreed to hand over Anni to the Dewani family and his parents vowed to accept our daughter as their own.

The priest tied Shrien's scarf to Anni's sari and Shrien applied vermilion to Anni's hair parting to formally make her his bride and end the ceremony.

Both Anni and Shrien bowed to touch first my feet and Nilam's and then those of his parents as a mark of respect.

There were loud cheers and clapping as the ceremony came to an end and I felt a sense of relief that it was over, in my heart wishing the newlyweds the very best for a long, happy, healthy life together filled with laughter.

Anni and Shrien's car was seen off by both families. Her sisters held the car to "ransom", as is traditional, and blocked it from driving off. This is always done in a sense of fun and grooms have to dip into their pockets and pay off the women to move out of the way.

I was told that Ami and Sneha were given 500 rupees each (around £5) while the other cousins were given 11 rupees by Shrien (11 pence).

Sneha later said that Anni had been desperate to go to the bathroom throughout and was pleased when the car finally got moving, although it only circled the hotel because the couple were spending their wedding night at the Renaissance. I had tears in my eyes again as I waved Anni off. My sentimentality regularly gets the better of me.

Later some of the youngsters headed for a nightclub and I took some friends to Sneha's suite, as arranged, to finish off the whisky and carry on celebrating.

I was surprised to find that Sneha had already gone to bed. She emerged from the bedroom and said she had been so tired out by the wedding that she could not keep her eyes open. She was determined that we still used the reception room of the suite, as long as we didn't disturb her sleep.

At around midnight Sneha came out of her room and rushed out of the suite. I was puzzled at the time but didn't think too much of it. I later discovered that Sneha had packed Anni's bag for her wedding night and left it at the reception, requesting that it be delivered to the hotel's wedding suite.

But it hadn't been sent up and remained instead by the reception causing Anni to make a frantic phone call to Sneha asking that she find the bag and deliver it personally in case it went missing again.

Sneha intended to hand over the bag through the half open door, but Shrien said: "Oh come in, come in." Of course she didn't want to disturb them on the wedding night but was pressured by Shrien to stay.

Sneha helped Anni fold her sari and put it away and asked her if they had managed to consummate the marriage. Anni responded by reminding her again that the couple were just going through the motions.

Sneha tried to leave, saying it was past midnight and she was sleepy, but Shrien and Anni were going to the restaurant as they were hungry and he asked her to join them as they walked to the elevator.

Sneha replied: "I am not going to join you. This is your wedding night. This is getting really weird now. You guys need to sort your issues out. I am going."

But to try to take the tension out of the moment, Sneha joked: "And stop treating me like your coolie. Get your own bags next time."

The Dewanis staged their reception the next evening. Anni looked fabulous in a blue sari and Sneha wore a matching one. Shrien helped fix her sari as she put it on. Anni told Sneha that Shrien even helped his own mother wrap her sari properly. Ashok's wife was also impressed by the way Shrien helped with her sari.

Saris are made from dozens of lengths of silk and women say they can be difficult to get right without help. Shrien seemed to be an expert at this.

The reception was also a really nice event. Shrien and Anni had their first dance as husband and wife. The lights were dimmed and, once again, I looked on with pride at such a beautiful couple. Shrien went down on one knee and Anni twirled away in a cleverly choreographed routine which brought loud cheers.

There were plentiful bottles of whisky which I had imported.

We also bought dozens and dozens of Anni's favourite Laurent-Perrier pink champagne for the toast and extra supplies of Shrien's preferred vodka, which he liked to drink with Diet Coke. The dinner was outstanding and the feast went down well with all.

The next morning Nilam and I were leaving for a short trip around India before heading back to Mariestad. Despite the smiles and laughter of the last few days I still had a very uncomfortable feeling about Anni and even had a fleeting urge to take her with us on our travels.

Sneha was worried and informed us about what had happened on Anni's wedding night and the fact that the couple had not slept together. Anni had also told Sneha she had gone ahead with the marriage because she felt that maybe she could sort everything out once they returned from India. She hoped that when they got home Shrien would be as funny and loving as he was when she first met him. She did love him but was unsure about so many things. She had question after question in her head.

I also clung to the hope that things would be settled once they were back home. Weddings are a very stressful time full stop and Anni was in a foreign country planning it all.

Anni came to the reception area and hugged and kissed us before waving us farewell. I had a heavy heart leaving her behind. Like Sneha, I was worried about the couple. But I hoped they would sort through their differences and that a good honeymoon, with time alone together, would afford them the space they needed. Surely their love would win.

That was the most important thing.

Anni said no honeymoon destination had been decided and that she was going to try to persuade Shrien to take her to Kerala which she had heard was beautiful.

We cried during our goodbyes but Anni asked me not to worry. Even though she would be living in the UK when she returned, it wasn't that far from Sweden and she promised we would still see a lot of each other.

I looked back at her as she waved. I treasure that last glorious smile she gave us because that was the very last time I saw my daughter alive.

Chapter 17

A surprise revelation

London, England
January 20, 2011

By the time Shrien was due to make his court appearance on January 20, 2011, at City of Westminster Magistrates' Court, the world's media were ready and waiting.

As I had insisted all along in telephone calls to each member of the Hindocha family, we were not to make any comment at all on whether he was guilty or innocent. All we wanted was the truth of what had happened to Anni and that should remain our only view on the matter.

Meanwhile various newspapers were running story after story questioning Shrien's alleged involvement in the case. I could just not stop myself from reading everything that was printed and floating around on social media.

When a Hindu priest from Shrien's locality said that my son-in-law wouldn't even harm a fly I began to feel very frustrated. I was sickened at the way people were talking about my daughter's murder while being oblivious to our feelings.

Meanwhile, Shrien's family and advisers began stating that he would return to South Africa if he was promised bail right up to a final appeal, if that was required. I found it incredible that he was thinking only of himself and this stretched as far ahead as any post-guilty verdict.

We felt he should be packing his case, going right back to Cape Town and sorting out who killed his wife and why. But his team wanted "a mutually agreed programme" before he went anywhere.

This infuriated me. I could not understand why Shrien was trying to negotiate his way around a properly constituted justice system which had been used and tested against so many other suspects. I could not understand why he was demanding special treatment. If he wanted bail, then he should walk into the dock at Cape Town court and plead his case like everybody else.

Surely Shrien should have been in a hurry to clear his name and put the people who had done this to the "love of his life" behind bars. Surely he wanted justice for her as quickly as possible. I didn't understand.

By now I just wanted the whole thing to begin moving. I needed a quick closure but there was no way I could demand it if the South Africans and the Dewanis were so far away from getting him on to a plane.

The day before the first London hearing, I read that Bheki Cele, the national police commissioner in South Africa, revealed police had established a motive for Anni's murder. I didn't know how. We were all none the wiser. There couldn't have been a financial motive because there was no life insurance or dowry in place on Anni, and Shrien wouldn't be part of a gang set up to rob his own wife of simple things such as a mobile phone, camera and jewellery and allow her to be shot.

When the day of Shrien's scheduled appearance before the court in London came about, he was nowhere to be seen.

I had flown from Gothenburg airport in Sweden with Nilam the night before and was settling down for dinner. The talk was all about the case. That's when we heard Shrien had fallen ill and would not be appearing before the court after all.

His case was adjourned in his absence for a month and we prepared to return home without knowing anything new.

Despite the charge against him, our first concerns were that he would recover quickly. Nobody would wish ill health on another person.

I was told Shrien had developed "acute stress disorder" and was too ill to attend the court. There was a sense of disappointment among us as we were becoming anxious that he should return to South Africa and help close the case as quickly as possible.

We did debate whether it was the loss of Anni or the charge against him which had caused him the biggest stress or a combination of both. It was important that we kept a sense of balance and fairness about everything to do with him, despite his near poisonous behaviour at times. There would be a huge spotlight on us throughout the whole case and we had to be careful not to be seen to interfere in the process of justice.

But in my own private thoughts I was loathing the way it was becoming all about Shrien. It should not have been like this. It should have been all about Anni, the girl that was actually murdered, and I was worried about her good name getting lost in all the sympathy being sought for her husband, now accused of her murder.

I tried hard to continue as normal during this period, but

I found it difficult to concentrate on my work, carrying out
electrical and engineering work for the Swedish contractors
who regularly call upon me to help them out. It was not easy.
Nothing was normal any more. I went to see a doctor. He
put me on sick leave for an initial period of three months.
I couldn't concentrate on my work anyway, my mind was
always on Anni and the case.

The suspicion of Shrien and now the clamour for everybody
to feel sorry for him disturbed my sleep night after night. The
loss of Anni seemed to be overshadowed by the Dewanis'
fears for his wellbeing. An article appeared in the Observer
newspaper describing how "fragile" Shrien was and that he
was suffering from flashbacks.

I ranted all day after seeing it because in our lives we
had to cope with a lot more than just flashbacks. We were
contaminated by the vision of Anni being shot dead by those
repulsive characters. It stayed with us 24/7. I called Ashok
to my home and he once again helped restore my sanity
and calm by assuring me that the South Africans were doing
everything possible to bring Shrien to trial and the whole
nightmare to a quick end.

I returned to Ashok's house and sat with my mother Ba,
who always has words of consolation and prayer. She has
been a constant tranquil influence on my life. I don't normally
go a day without seeing her when we are in Mariestad. My
children and the rest of the family have an enormous amount
of respect for her. All of us, from my eldest brother Jayanti to
my youngest grandchild, owe her everything for making us the
loving and trusting family we are. Ba always has good advice
and kept telling me that I should have faith, that God was with

us. She was a great source of comfort at the time.

Anni used to look up to her both as a child and as a young woman. Ba was her carer and nurtured her, teaching her about our religion and how Anni should present herself. They spent many days together over the years and were very close. I worried about Ba too and how she was dealing with her own sadness.

Ashok and I could not help ourselves continually discussing exactly what the police suspected was the motive for Shrien to mastermind Anni's murder just a few weeks after marrying her.

We pondered if the police would be claiming that Shrien had another woman in his life or if he had been blackmailed into participating in the murder. We were speculating a lot around this topic.

The answer of why police thought Shrien may have been driven to murder Anni came in the shape of a man called Leopold Leisser, a male prostitute.

He went under the nickname of The German Master and his identity was revealed by the journalist Nick Parker, who was to play a key role in the prosecution much later.

Ashok and I typed "German Master" into Google and were surprised to see what was there. A photograph appeared showing him wearing a leather cap and outfit, smoking a cigar.

The German Master boasted about his "uncut 8 inch tool." The "Master's stats" showed that he was 6.1ft tall, weighed 105kg, had a hairy body and full trimmed beard.

The "Master's equipment" was there for all to see in photographs and showed an array of sexual aids such as handcuffs, blindfolds, pliers, mangles, dildos, stocks, slings, gags, nipple devices, and a paddle and whips – most of which I didn't recognise.

This gentleman was being questioned by police over his claim that Shrien had paid him for sex. Furthermore, the bill was £1,100 for three gay sessions with Shrien. The German Master had signed a statement with police and would be giving evidence.

I have to state here and now that I do not have anything against homosexuality if it involves consenting adults and do not believe a person should be defined by their sexuality. Each to their own. But I believe most people would agree that my utter shock and distaste at this development were understandable. I hit the roof and swore like never before. My profanities must have been audible in every nearby home as I unleashed my anger and utter disgust at Shrien.

Sleeping with male prostitutes? Paying for sex? And then sharing a bed with my beloved and unsuspecting Anni. How on earth could I have missed this? Why did I not see the warning signs?

My poor, poor Anni. She would not have known about this and she would never have married him had she known about his sordid secrets.

My anger was fuelled when I thought about other men buggering the German Master and the danger of Shrien passing on an infection to my daughter. How dirty and obscene the whole thing had become. Had he always been careful to practise safe sex while indulging himself with these men?

I was aware that sex had been minimal between Anni and

her husband because of all the health problems Shrien had experienced. But now, at last, I had an explanation.

Shrien was apparently gay. He preferred men to women. He was into sleeping with other men and he had kept it all secret.

Everything appeared to fall into place. The so-called fertility problems, the statement of being against sex before marriage and the avoidance of my family and friends on all but two occasions before the marriage.

He had pushed Anni away repeatedly, shunned her in a way that made her feel ugly and unwanted. Anni had confided in Sneha that Shrien had problems getting an erection and this had been put down to his health.

We wondered now if it was because he was gay and simply didn't fancy women, no matter how beautiful they were.

He must have been worried that his secret would be uncovered by one of us and that is why he kept his distance.

My family went into further shock and Nilam, who I thought could cry no more, was in floods of tears when I informed her of the latest turn of events.

Some of the younger Hindochas began saying they hated Shrien and mocked him because of his depravity. I was just wounded. Guilt riddled my heart. I had given my daughter to this cold-hearted excuse for a man. She had died alone in a car with gunmen. She must have screamed for her life and this husband of hers had not been there for her in her hour of need. He had deceived me and many others, but most of all Anni.

What had driven him to marry such a beautiful young woman who had so much to live for and would have been the cherished princess on the arm of millions of other men, given the chance? Which other men had he been sleeping with and who else knew about this before he became my daughter's husband?

Sneha and Ami, who were Anni's closest confidantes, declared they knew nothing about Shrien being gay. They both stated that if Anni had known about his contemptible lifestyle she would have brought her relationship with him to an abrupt end. If these two women were not informed by Anni about Shrien's squalid connections, then Anni most certainly had not known.

I was unsure whether it was the filthy behaviour with gay prostitutes or the deception of it all that hurt me most. But I was hurt and feeling completely swindled by Shrien Dewani.

It wasn't going to be easy telling Ba the truth about him. The marriage was now so obviously a sham, and people love a good scandal. It is the way of the world.

All of my lovely friends and guests who had honoured us by travelling to India would soon be learning of this unpleasant news and I hoped they would not be offended by being dragged into this fake marriage. They had given us their goodwill and I very much appreciated that.

Ashok and I spent hours considering all the reasons why a gay man would marry a girl and deceive her in such a way. Firstly we put it down to the fact that Shrien was from a conservative Hindu family where conformity would have been of prime importance. Shrien may not have been able to tell his family out of fear or respect.

I could not see how Prakash, Shrien's father, would have known about his son's homosexuality and liaisons with male prostitutes.

In my troubled mind, many ideas circled and moved around. But my darkest thought was for the person at the centre of it all, Anni.

This innocent young woman had gone into her marriage hoping to be loved and cherished. She gave her mind, body and soul to her husband and all the time he had lied to her. It was inexplicable that she should end up in his hands. Anni gave only love and had such a kind and trusting heart.

I began to question my own judgment over whether Anni might have felt pushed into the marriage herself, given all her doubts about Shrien and the problems they had. The whole family wanted nothing but her happiness and for her to have a stable future with her husband and the children she would have adored. Possibly she could have felt pressured to go through with it because of the burden of expectation and with all the money spent and the invitations sent out... If only I had been able to put a stop to it all, Anni would still be alive.

Sneha gave me words of comfort when she insisted that Anni was in love with Shrien, who had made her laugh and laugh. She had hoped that after their wedding and all the tensions that pervaded their relationship, she might be able to recapture the good times and build on them in marriage.

I was well aware that marriages can fail. Had Anni lived long enough to decide life with Shrien wasn't for her, she would have known we would have supported her through a divorce.

Chapter 18

A mother's instinct

Mariestad, Sweden
November, 2010

The weeks after the wedding were difficult. Anni had been living away from home in London so we had got used to not seeing her but I was still getting accustomed to the fact she now belonged to another man and was his wife.

I challenge any father who has seen his daughter get married to deny he felt the same way I did. I thought about my youngest daughter day and night, about how she was getting on with Shrien's parents Prakash and Shila and whether they were like a new father and mother to Anni.

I had been disappointed with certain aspects of the wedding but it was time to move on. Anni was a wife and her future had been sealed with Shrien. Above all I wished them a long and happy life together. I hoped the differences they'd had during the engagement would soon be forgotten.

There were some obvious questions I thought about regularly. What was her day like? How did she spend her hours? What were meal times like with her new family? Simple things buzzed through my mind as I returned to daily life in Mariestad, playing golf and doing bits of electrical and engineering work whenever I could.

Nilam resumed her long morning walks and seeing her friends in the afternoon and we talked about Anni each night, remembering the wedding, mostly with smiles.

Mariestad is a small town with a population of around 16,000 and news of the wedding had filtered through to the people who run the stalls in the market square opposite the Stadt Hotel, which had been owned by Ashok for a couple of years by that time.

They would stop and congratulate us. Most had known Anni since she was a baby and had seen her going to school, playing on the swings near Lake Vänern and, as a teenager, drinking coffee with friends and cousins in the cafes. She had grown up with their children and Anni was one of their own. Some would ask to see photographs of Anni in her wedding sari and I was always more than happy to oblige.

I suppose I had buried my anxieties about Anni's unease with Shrien in order to ensure she had a smooth passage into the Dewani family. I had never broached the subject with Prakash. I did not want to risk upsetting the Dewanis in case it made them feel my Anni wasn't good enough for their son. I know that is ridiculous, as she was an amazingly bright and beautiful young woman, but all I wanted was happiness for Anni and for her to marry the man she wanted.

I was aware that Shrien had been engaged before and had broken it off. I'd heard that he had said his ex-fiancée did not fit into his family. I did not want him to leave Anni as well and had to watch my words very carefully. I still didn't know whether the Dewanis were aware of the tensions, the rows and the calling off of the engagement before Anni got back together with Shrien.

But I had instilled a strong sense of duty and respect in my children which, in this case, I hoped would help Anni overcome any problems and win over her new family. She would shine and light up their household, just like she did ours and, indeed, any home wherever she went. Her sunny cheerfulness and natural, caring disposition would win anybody over.

With my eldest daughter Ami there had never been any concerns about her husband as she had quickly fallen deeply in love with him and they never appeared anything but happy.

We are a genuinely loving family and there has never been a hint of conflict among us. We live in a small town where I can't remember any real crime or violence. Sure, the youngsters fall out sometimes, but any arguments are always solved within a short period of time. Shrien was immediately accepted into the fold as one of us.

We hadn't heard from Anni in a couple of days. Nilam and I were fine about that as we just had to get used to her being with her new family. I learned through the Hindocha grapevine that she and Shrien had returned safely to Bristol from India on November 3.

Anni called home during Diwali, the Indian light festival, to wish us a prosperous new year. About a week later we heard that the couple had gone to South Africa on honeymoon. Nilam received a telephone call from Sneha but nobody from Shrien's family called us.

Sneha told us they were going to the Kruger National Park. I thought that was great. Anni deserved to be pampered and to enjoy a special honeymoon after all the stress of the wedding. I checked the place out on the internet and saw that it was a huge safari park. The weather was also good there and I was happy. She would love the fine weather and seeing all the animals.

Nilam and I thought it best to give Anni time to settle down with Shrien before we made contact. I told Nilam we should give it a few weeks or wait until Anni contacted us. We didn't want to be seen as interfering in-laws and they were on their honeymoon.

On Saturday, November 13, Nilam was very troubled. She kept asking me: "Shall we call Anni?" She repeated it several times that day.

Nilam said she was feeling depressed, that she was missing Anni a lot and wanted to know that everything was okay with her. I now believe it was a mother's instinct that something was wrong.

Every Saturday evening I would play volleyball with friends from 7.30 until 10pm. Despite my previous resolution I relented and told Nilam that I would call Anni before I went to play volleyball.

At about 6.30pm Swedish time, which was 7.30pm in South Africa, I dialled Shrien's number and he answered. He said they were having a nice time in Cape Town and everything was fine. I said I wanted to talk to Anni but he said he wasn't with her as he was in the town changing money. I asked him why he was exchanging money in the town.

"Don't you have facilities in the hotel?" was my question.

There was silence for a few seconds and then he said: "Yeah, we have that in the hotel but it is cheaper to do it here on the black market. You get a better rate."

I told him again that I would like to speak with Anni and he said he would ask her to call me when he got back to the hotel.

At around 7.15pm my home line rang and it was Shrien. He didn't greet me or ask me how I was but simply said: "Anni is here."

It was so lovely to hear her voice. I had missed her so much already. The last time I had seen her was in Mumbai. She had since been to the UK and now she had surfaced in South Africa.

There was so much catching up to do but my main purpose in speaking to her was to establish that she was fine and to reassure her worried mother.

She started talking to me in Gujarati and said: "Papa, South Africa is so lovely we are having a very nice time. I could move here."

Then for a reason that I could not immediately work out, she started talking in Swedish and I realised Shrien was with her and she didn't want him to understand what she was saying.

She said (in Swedish): "Pappa, jag har jättemycket att berätta, Vi tar det på tisdag när jag är tillbaks i England.

(Papa, I have so much to tell you. But I'll tell you on Tuesday when I get back to England)."

Her tone was anxious and worried.

I asked her in Swedish: "Är allt OK?" (Is everything OK?).

She responded, also in Swedish: "Jag ska berätta för er på tisdag." (I'll tell you on Tuesday).

I said: "Anni, vi älskar dig." (Anni, we love you) and told her I was going to play volleyball.

I handed the telephone to Nilam as I was running late for

ANNI: A FATHER'S STORY

the game. Anni said the same words in Swedish to Nilam – that she had so much to tell her and would speak to her on the following Tuesday. It was a very short chat and the call ended.

Anni had been my daughter for 28 years and I would definitely know what she was feeling by her tone. I had never had a call like that one.

I was a little disturbed as I drove off. When I normally talked with Anni she was full of affection and showed a deep interest in what was going on. She could take 30 minutes inquiring about each and every member of the family. This time she was hesitant and I couldn't understand why. When the line went dead I was upset. Firstly about her putting the telephone down so suddenly, but then I began to worry about her. I sensed something was wrong.

Shrien was standing next to her as he had dialled my number and handed her the phone when I answered.

I wondered why would she suddenly switch to Swedish. Did she not want him to hear what she was about to say? She had said she was having a good time and that gave me some assurance, but why the secrecy? Anni wasn't the type of person to lie and speak badly about others and, after all, this was her husband. I wondered if the pre-wedding tension had come back and that she wanted to discuss it. It bothered me and I was puzzled.

But I comforted myself that it was Saturday and she would be back in England on Tuesday. That wasn't long to wait to speak with her properly.

It was good to see my old volleyball friends. They were also victims of the Idi Amin expulsion from Uganda, and this had forged a close bond between us. There were 18 of us that night and we enjoyed the game as normal. It is my way of keeping fit as I move through my sixties. The evening helped take my mind off the call for a while.

When I got home I watched TV with Nilam. I think it was a movie, but such was the worry in my mind over Anni's anxiety that I didn't take much in and cannot recall what the movie was called or even what it was about.

Nilam and I spoke briefly about the phone call, hoping that Anni would have a good last few days in South Africa and reach home safely, ready to talk to us frankly about what was bothering her.

As I rested my head on my pillow around midnight and fell asleep, I could never have known that evening was to have been the last time I would hear Anni's voice.

The phone woke me shortly afterwards.

Chapter 19

Lengthy delays and agonising frustrations

London, England
February, 2011

Proceedings were moving much faster in South Africa than in London. My days became filled with dealing with the media, maintaining contact with Scotland Yard and trawling the internet for the latest developments and bits of information.

Meanwhile in Cape Town's Wynberg Magistrates' Court, Qwabe told how he had been recruited to kill Anni and stage a fake car-jacking. He said he had released Shrien before driving Anni off to murder her.

He accused his accomplice Xolie Mngeni of shooting Anni and said both had been hired along with Zola Tongo. Police had recovered the cartridge from the bullet which had been fired at Anni.

It was some consolation to see that justice was moving pretty fast in South Africa, in comparison with the UK, but it still hit us hard when we discovered that Anni's possessions had been recovered from the hitmen too.

My mood was growing darker by the day. I was finding it more and more difficult not to snap and speak my mind, even

though I berated my own family if they did so. I was ordered
by Ashok to watch my words carefully, particularly in public.

At Shrien's next scheduled hearing in early February he
failed to show yet again and once more blamed mental illness.
This time I lost it and walked into a storm of my own. But I
did not regret telling the South African press that I had heard
rumours that he had been seen in restaurants in the Bristol
area and therefore should be able to participate in court
proceedings.

Of course these remarks duly appeared in the UK press and
I noted that some newspapers said I'd been fiercely criticised
for accusing him of faking his mental illness. I was frustrated.
How can things take so long? It had been three months
already and nothing had happened in the the British courts
that would have Shrien extradited. At this point, I couldn't
even in my wildest imagination have predicted just how long
the road for seeking justice would turn out to be.

Nevertheless the judge at Woolwich Crown Court in
London adjourned the case and ordered Shrien to appear the
next time on March 23. We hoped not to have a third wasted
journey.

The judge also decided a full extradition hearing would
begin on May 3 and I hoped it would not be very long before
I saw Shrien put on a plane and returned to Cape Town.

If my frustration was high at the slow turning of the wheels
of justice in London, then my angry state of mind grew
even worse as I learned that the two gangsters, Qwabe and
Mngeni, were now accusing police of beating them up to elicit
their confessions. Was it true or not? How can you know for
sure? I was confused and didn't know what to believe about

this new information.

After thinking about it non stop I realized that this was bad news. I sat in the front room of my home, held my head in my hands and sobbed like a child. We were being given good news with one hand and bad news with the other as each day passed. These two men had claimed they were beaten with a heavy torch, punched and suffocated with a plastic bag before they admitted their roles in Anni's murder.

My knowledge of how lawyers worked was minimal but even I could see that they would jump on this and say these people should be freed because the police were trying to frame them.

Their complex case was bound to be studied by a top drawer legal team working for Shrien in London and used to show that it would be unsafe to send him back as he too might fall into a corrupt legal system and be wrongly convicted.

The two suspects were asking their lawyers in Cape Town to re-class their previous confessions as merely statements rather than admissions. I was even more confused. All I knew was that it meant bad news all round for getting on with the case and making sure Shrien went back to South Africa, so that the truth of what happened that night could be revealed – once and for all.

I'd been told that there were around 18,000 murders and 50,000 rapes each year in South Africa. Violence was rife. But these figures, combined with the pressure on police to solve crimes, were certain to be used by Shrien to try to prevent Judge Riddle from sending him back and allowing us access to his version of what happened on the night of November 13, 2010.

Ashok was reported to have said that these events were "rubbing salt into our wounds." Forgive me, brother, but that was an understatement if ever I heard one.

Around the same time I learned that Shrien would be taking legal action over the claims that he was a homosexual or had any involvement with The German Master. His denials had come from Max Clifford.

I warned my family never to speak about or discuss the male prostitute claims publicly, as we were now walking through a legal minefield.

Remarks by Menzi Simelane, an advocate and director of the South African National Prosecuting Authority, were also seized upon after he described Shrien as a "guilty fugitive."

It would all fuel Shrien's claim that he would not receive a fair trial in South Africa and my role in the whole affair was becoming less and less important.

While the sides looked to gain advantage for their cases, my family and I were stuck in the middle. We were being reduced to a small dot on the map between Cape Town and London. My pain was deepening each day. My blood pressure was rising and Nilam's health was deteriorating. We were just not feeling well.

In one of her texts to a friend in India, Anni talked of crying being her new hobby. Now it was ours too as we tried frantically to get a hold on what was going on.

Day after day came more hurtful news, when all we wanted was the truth and the chance to move on and mourn Anni properly without being under scrutiny.

What we learned in late February 2011 was another knife into an already deep, open wound. It was claimed that "powerful new evidence" had been uncovered in Cape Town proving Anni was sexually assaulted by the hitmen. This went against all the assurances I had been given by the South African police. That day quickly became one of the worst since my daughter had been taken.

This revelation could cast doubt on police claims that Anni was the victim of a pre-planned car-jacking, which was tough enough to deal with. But how was I to live with the fact that my daughter was violated? And why had the police assured me differently to my face in Cape Town?

I was straight on to the telephone to the prosecutors in Cape Town and was beyond relieved by their assurances the stories were untrue and probably placed to muddy the waters when it came to the trials.

You can only begin to imagine the turmoil in my household and throughout the entire Hindocha family during this time. Our emotions were being shuffled like a pack of cards and it all just seemed very unfair on us.

When a tragedy hits, I believe police forces and social workers provide emotional support to see families through the difficult days ahead. Our problem was that we were in Sweden and there could be no accurate way to assess how long this miserable process of getting Shrien back to South Africa to face trial could take.

I had to be strong for Nilam, for my son and daughter and for everybody. Although I tried my level best, at times it was too much for me. I would try to disappear and walk around Mariestad in the hope that the solitude would help me deal with the psychological warfare within me.

I was also racked with guilt over the loss of Anni and being unable to protect her in her moment of need. Everywhere I looked, there was a reminder of my innocent girl.

Over there were the swings that I would push her on and nearby was Lake Vänern where we used to enjoy strolling together and chatting. Around the corner was her nursery school. If I walked into town there was the market square where she loved strolling around the shops. Everybody knew her and loved her. People were mostly too polite to acknowledge me now, as they must have believed they would be intruding on my grief. Those who did stop me had nothing but beautiful things to say about Anni. Yet none of us could have helped her on that godforsaken night in Gugulethu.

Returning home would always bring me back to the same sad scenario. Nilam would be lying depressed in bed and I would sit on the sofa, staring at the floor. We both lost weight because our interest in eating had disappeared. The only appetite we really had was for the truth. My son and Ashok were enormous pillars of strength and I admired them both, whenever I could think clearly. Anish was only 22 and he had been incredibly close to Anni. He showed a strength and maturity way beyond his years.

Ashok was Anni's fun uncle and loved her like his own daughter. She respected him and the uncle and niece were always joking together and teasing each other. Now there was a void and the only thing that helped us get through it was the determination to win justice for Anni.

The South Africans advised us not to read the daily newspaper reports and definitely not to believe much of what we read.

But the desperate need for the latest news became a

necessity, whether it was informative or irritating, I wanted to know everything so I read everything. Inevitably I would Google using the keyword "Dewani" and sometimes the daily hit rate could reach 250-500 articles.

I was introduced to the relatively new phenomenon of the internet troll, which brings out the nasty side of people across the world at the touch of a keyboard. These people did not know Anni or, to be fair, Shrien, and their remarks were both extremely hurtful and unwarranted.

Although I was not speaking with the Dewanis, given their son was being accused of murdering my daughter, I did think about picking up the telephone when it was revealed in banner front page headlines that Shrien had tried to commit suicide.

If he had, indeed, attempted to take his own life and succeeded, that would have just been another tragic stage in the whole sorry affair. It would also have meant that we might never know what part, if any at all, he played in Anni's death.

Shrien was said to have taken an overdose of pills and been rushed to hospital where he'd been detained. He had acted disgracefully after Anni's death and I would probably never be able to forgive him for that. But I didn't want another life to be lost and his father to experience the same daily turmoil.

I decided against contacting the family after seeking the advice of Ashok and Jayanti. We agreed that, although the gesture was genuine, it could be wrongly interpreted by the Dewanis as interference.

Fortunately Shrien survived and was released after a few days and returned home to his family. They said he had suffered a reaction to his medication and it was not an attempt

to commit suicide. This information came from Clifford so
was to be treated with caution. But it was an indication of the
stress that the Dewanis were suffering too.

We were to get our first glimpse of Shrien in a British court
at the third attempt, when he finally appeared at Belmarsh
Magistrates' Court on February 24, 2011.

The court was in an unremarkable suburb of South London
and we spent hours trying to work out how to locate and travel
to it. We arrived en masse with about 15-20 Hindochas there
to see the process of sending Shrien back to South Africa
begin.

Shrien looked disheveled and had grown an unflattering
beard. When he entered the dock, which could easily have
housed a dozen suspects, he stared down at the ground,
declining to make eye contact with me, or anyone.

The lawyer that represented the South African authorities
raised the matter of the overdose. He said that if Shrien was
suffering from significant mental health problems he should be
placed in custody for his own protection and to reduce the risk
of him absconding.

Shrien's legal team denied the suicide bid and Judge
Riddle said he needed a second opinion on his mental state.
Shrien wanted to stay at home with his family and not to be
remanded in hospital.

Prakash was in tears as he pleaded with the court to
allow his son to remain at home while the case proceeded,
promising to do everything to protect him from any attempt
to take his own life.

As I sat there listening to the arguments and thinking how
much brain power, money and time was being spent on

Shrien's wellbeing, I could not help returning to the central theme in my mind... What about my Anni? Where did she fit into all this? I don't remember any mention of her name and she appeared to have been lost in this legal wrangling.

But it was Anni who had lost her life. There was no need for skirting around the issue. This man was accused of murdering my daughter and all he had to do was take a 12-hour flight to Cape Town and simply tell the truth. If he was innocent he had nothing to fear. What about us all getting up and boarding a plane to South Africa right now and showing her memory the respect due by getting to the bottom of what happened that night?

Chapter 20

Gugulethu

Cape Town, South Africa
February, 2011

My family understood how difficult it was for me to remain at home in Mariestad while the planning and organisation of trying the suspects continued in South Africa.

I wanted, needed, to be closer to the investigation and to know and understand what was going on as Shrien did his best to avoid extradition.

After intense family discussions, everybody agreed it would be easier if Nilam and I went to see for ourselves how things were progressing in South Africa. There was little I could do at home, and the distance and problems with communicating between the two countries were only compounding the pain. Information was being lost in translation and I felt my presence would confirm to the South Africans that I was intending to be involved and informed as fully as possible until the case had been concluded.

We made a short trip back to Cape Town in late February to see Qwabe and Mngeni appear before the court there.

The South African prosecutors were extremely helpful and comforting – assuring us that the two men in custody were the right suspects and they too would soon join Tongo in being locked up for a long, long time.

When they appeared for separate hearings at Wynberg Court from a staircase underneath the dock and took their places, I could not help myself. I broke down and wept in front of the magistrate, the prosecution, the defence, the media, the police and all the others who had attended.

They were not just tears of anger, or hatred towards these two individuals. I wept also for my daughter as the sight of these two men made me see her ending in a whole new light. I looked at their faces and developed a mental picture of their eyes as they took Anni's life. Had they been laughing as they killed her? Theirs were the last faces on earth she would see. They had admitted killing her and Anni's possessions had been recovered from them. In a split second they ended Anni's life. And, yes, once they had been found guilty I wanted their freedom to be ended for ever too.

Mngeni was only a few feet away from me with rings in both ears. He appeared not to be bothered by the accusations put forward to him. He would not even look at me and showed no remorse.

Qwabe was a short man and, unlike Mngeni, he often looked up at the public gallery, paying attention to the people around him.

I had never come across men like these before. They had an air of menace about them and this had not been diminished by the serious charges they faced and the prospect of a lifetime in jail.

But I was not aware that photographers were in the courtroom and a picture of me, eyes closed and with tears streaming down my face as I held Anni's photograph, was on all the front pages the next day. It was to become an image that would be used countless times to illustrate the depth of the Hindocha family's grief and it was entirely accurate. We were totally grief-stricken.

The chief prosecution lawyer Rodney de Kock told the court that detectives needed more time and information from London. The hearing was told that Anni had been murdered at the behest of Shrien.

The trial of the two individuals had to be adjourned until his extradition hearing and Qwabe's lawyers argued that if Shrien was allowed his freedom on bail, then so should he.

At the age of 25, Qwabe was a father of three children and also supported their mother. He was refused bail and returned to prison. Mngeni was also sent back to jail to await trial on June 1.

The media penned me in outside the court, which I was not expecting. I told them: "I have come all the way from Sweden to see my daughter's murderers. I see things are going well in South Africa."

Nilam and I also visited the spot in Khayelitsha, Gugulethu, where Anni's body was found. It was important to us that we visited, no matter how hard. We were accompanied by a Hindu priest. It was another highly emotional day. I could not help but feel extremely sorry for my wife as she laid a heart-shaped wreath on the street where Tongo's
Volkswagen Sharan taxi had been abandoned with Anni's body lying across the back seat. No mother should have to go through such a thing.

It struck me what a remarkably quiet, nondescript road it

was where they had callously left the vehicle containing Anni, with houses and huts to one side and barren land on the other. There was about 30ft of shrubbery either side of the street and few passers-by.

Somehow the media homed in on our visit. Rather than feel intruded upon, I was happy that everyone accompanying us would be able to see the affection we had for our daughter. The wreath was symbolic in so many ways – a token of our grief as well as our outright love for her. I told reporters who had gathered that Shrien should also pray for Anni and I hoped every single day that he would return to Cape Town.

Nilam could not speak throughout the experience. She was completely silent except for her prayers.

We had brought with us a board displaying a photograph of Anni and messages from her close friends. Our message said: "From Mama, Papa, Ami and Anish."

As we knelt in front of Anni's picture and the priest prayed, Nilam and I held hands, whispering her name repeatedly, and then lit two candles.

Nilam's hands trembled as she unpinned the photograph of our daughter from her chest and placed it above the photograph on the wooden board. It was a gesture we would repeat many more times.

We had been told by police that Anni had eaten her last meal at the Surfside restaurant in Strand, a few miles away, so we drove there as we had to see the place.

I could not believe Anni would have wanted to go there when she was dressed up to the nines. I will never forget the dress she was wearing that last evening of her life. I had seen pictures and that dress summed up her stylish dress sense. It was a short black dress with gold straps on one shoulder, on the other shoulder she was wearing a shawl and, of course, she was wearing her beloved high heels.

I remember Shrien saying that she had her small clutch purse that evening. Anni always accessorised her dresses with these little purses. The funny thing is that these purses were all really nice but she could barely fit anything in them. I used to ask her why she would spend money on something she could not use practically and she always use to laugh at me and say: "Papa, it's fashion, you wouldn't understand!"

The Surfside was a welcoming place but I thought its fast seafood menu and location close to the beach was not exactly a suitable venue to take your wife for a romantic dinner on honeymoon. When Anni had gone out that night in her black evening dress she must have been expecting something more upmarket. Surfside was a place far out of Cape Town. I did not understand how they came to have dinner there.

Nilam was again sobbing and hugged me as we went to the corner table where Anni had sat and we looked out towards the sea, knowing that her beautiful eyes had also taken in this view. It was a tough, but necessary visit.

Back home, Shrien's mental condition was not improving and he was admitted to the Priory Hospital in Bristol for treatment and analysis. I was worried about him but I have to admit I was more concerned about Nilam and the family as the months were passing and there appeared to be no definite date for his return.

Shrien held the key to the whole story and he had to go back to Cape Town as soon as possible. I had to be strong and I was well supported by the family but there were so many dark moments. Sleep was impossible and the fatigue and stress were taking a great toll on me.

While Shrien had been placed on a 15 minute suicide watch at The Priory I longed for 15 minutes of peace.

His bid to find respite had been stalled when he was behind a disturbance at The Priory and, after police had been called, he had been transferred to the Cygnet Hospital in Kewstoke, Somerset. He had apparently suffered a reaction to his medication.

Many members of my family joined me from Sweden and the UK when Shrien made his next court appearance in London and I was thankful that he had been able to attend in person.

Shrien's family were on one side of the court and mine on the other as Judge Riddle took his place. He was extremely attentive and efficient as he extended Shrien's bail and listened to updated prosecution and defence submissions.

There was further drama when Shrien made an appearance at Westminster Magistrates' Court and fell to his knees after the hearing. Personally I thought it was a very dramatic gesture and was not convinced it hadn't been deliberate to gain sympathy. I knew I had to keep any negative thoughts about him deep down. One word out of place could add to the already frustrating delay.

The hearing had already been interrupted when Shrien fled from the dock holding his stomach as if in pain. He had mumbled to himself. He did not look well. I wasn't surprised. I later discussed with Ashok how few men would look well if they were accused of murder, particularly when they were wanted for killing their wife on honeymoon.

Privately we felt Shrien needed to man up and face his accusers. Publicly we were being very careful to refrain from saying anything against him except for our mantra that he needed to return to South Africa, explain what happened and give us closure.

Incredibly, he was quoted as talking about his own agony and suffering over Anni's death. We could not believe that he was speaking out and I established that a "friend" had been talking on his behalf. Apparently he had been saying: "No one wants to find out the truth more than me."

Shrien was so wrong. Nobody wanted the truth more than me, and Anni's mother, sister and brother. If he wanted to substantiate the truth, he had to play his part and tell all that he knew.

There was clearly a massive public relations operation working on Shrien's behalf and it was very cleverly organised. I could not put my finger on how it was being conducted. Max Clifford was the mouthpiece and a very potent one but the background machinery was well hidden from the surface. It was working, though, as sympathy for him seemed to be rising. Shrien was being presented as a man whose wife had been murdered and who was wrongly accused. His was an unfair situation with much of the world baying for his blood, hoping to see him dragged off to the cells and locked up for his lifetime.

In reality, things were very different. I had it in my power to turn his fortunes around immediately with a few words. I had only to brief the media on my suspicions and that would upset the applecart and negate all the PR hard work carried out on his behalf.

But I am cleverer than that and, I hope, fairer. After his disgraceful behaviour around Anni's body and his insensitive treatment of my family I saw the dark side to Shrien. I wasn't ever going to say he killed Anni but I wasn't his greatest fan or supporter by any stretch of the imagination. I still hoped he would get a fair trial. If I had chosen to I could have undone all the positive public relations rubbish he was enjoying. There wasn't a day that went by without requests for interviews from television presenters, authors and journalists.

Ashok, Jayanti and I had a meeting and agreed that we did not need to hire a public relations expert. We hoped people would see us for who we were, a family whose only mission was to establish the truth. Ashok said he would continue liaising with the media to keep Anni at the forefront and help expedite Shrien's return.

This period had, however, served to increase my anxiety even further. I knew the path to getting Shrien back to Cape Town was going to be a very complicated legal process, with all the usual procedures to be followed. I just never could have imagined the turn of events and the subsequent delays that were to come.

Chapter 21

A final farewell

Mariestad, Sweden
Saturday, May 14, 2011

The entire Hindocha family gathered to say our final farewell to Anni on Saturday, May 14, 2011, at Lake Vänern. Her sacred ashes were scattered where she had spent many days as a child, swimming and playing in the water and around its banks.

I had considered whether it would have been more suitable to take her ashes to India for scattering in the holy River Ganges, as is traditional for many Hindus. But it felt more natural to place her remains in the lake she had always been happy in, Lake Vänern in Mariestad.

I wanted to be close to her in some way and be able to feel her presence whenever I wandered by. The same went for the rest of my family. They all wanted her close.

Six months had now passed since her brutal death. Before that I had looked at her as a proud father as she walked in front of me, resplendent in her wedding sari, to begin the next stage of her life.

Now her life was over. As I held the urn in both hands and tipped her remains into the water, I still had to ask myself if this really was true or a nightmare that I might wake up from in any minute.

In just six months, I had gone from being one of the happiest and proudest fathers in the world to the most heartbroken. Evil had pervaded my life and I could not have prepared for it. Financial problems, health or business worries or even violence against me, yes. Those are troubles you spend your life hoping never come your way, but for which you have a back-up plan if they do strike.

But murder, and that of your child too? Nothing could ever be prescribed to remedy the total feeling of loss and guilt that inflicts a father who has lost a daughter in such a way. I had repeatedly told family members I would have swapped places with Anni and readily given my life to save hers. With the help of Ashok and Jayanti and the three children, Nilam would have coped eventually if it had been my life.

Yet there was only one Anni. She was irreplaceable and it hit me repeatedly throughout this solemn ceremony – we shouldn't be doing this.

My despair was deepened by seeing Ba seated opposite me, looking sad beyond words, on the tiny boat we had hired to take us to the centre of the lake. It was soothing seeing her there because she was my mother, and the sight of her always gave me confidence and a feeling of wellbeing. Now here she was, watching her son put her granddaughter's ashes into the water. The script was not meant to be like this. What would it do to the head of our family, who was approaching her nineties and had protected Anni, guided her and helped mould her into the beautiful young woman she had become?

That sunny morning we were grieving as one. All of us

were dressed in white, as is the custom at a time of Hindu mourning. It is meant to be the colour of purity.

Ashok had invited a team from Channel 4's Dispatches programme to film the scattering of Anni's ashes. They were making a documentary called Murder on Honeymoon, which was to be an investigation into Anni's death. The documentary producer had approached Ashok with great sensitivity and we had agreed we should help. Anything that might give us the information that we still craved. They were in their own boat and kept their distance, as agreed.

There was never going to be any question of inviting Shrien or any of the Dewanis to the ceremony after the trauma of the pizza party and his terrible conduct at the funeral.

I felt the two families were as far apart as could be, in complete contrast to the wedding day back in Mumbai. Some might have advised me that Anni's husband had some sort of right to attend the ceremony. But this was never going to happen.

We had felt humiliated and marginalised by Shrien's performance at Anni's funeral in London. Nilam will always be bitter that he could not even grant her a few minutes alone with her daughter's body. I should have demanded that but at that time everything was moving too fast and I was not in the right frame of mind. There are so many times I wish I could just turn back time.

I didn't want any more dramas and certainly not in my home town. Shrien could not be trusted to keep the peace. He was mentally unwell and stood accused of murdering Anni. It would not have been right to include him.

This was the Hindochas moment to say goodbye to our

Anni. We wanted and needed the purity of it to be respected.
She had been ours for 28 years and theirs for merely a few
weeks. Her family demanded this.

We wore her picture on our clothing and prayed for her
soul as we dropped flower petals into the water, taking turns
to hold the urn and let Anni's remains fall into the water. My
heart also fell away along with her ashes.

There were few of us who could hold back the tears. The
women hugged each other and sobbed loudly for Anni. It was
left to Ashok to find the fitting words for the television cameras
when he said Anni would not be at peace until the full story of
how she was murdered had been confirmed.

We did take some solace from the fact that Anni would
always be here in her home town, where she had enjoyed an
innocent childhood and a steady path into womanhood.
Where she had spent sunny days and where she belonged.

After the ashes were spread we went home for family
prayers. Some of my closest friends joined to show their
respect. There was a very calm and peaceful atmosphere
despite the intense sadness. It was comforting to know that my
family was there for me and that we all were strong and
united during this difficult time.

Despite the circumstances it had been a beautiful ceremony,
full of respect and love for Anni. But my day was later spoiled
when a journalist reported once again that Anni may have
been sexually attacked. The timing of this article was just
horrible and we later made sure the newspaper printed a
clarification that there had been no such attack on her.

The process of bringing her husband to trial was still
grindingly slow and there was a major obstacle in the trial of

the two men in South Africa.

Mngeni had suffered health problems, namely a brain tumour, and had undergone two operations. He had collapsed in his cell. This was seen as a boost for Shrien and would probably delay his extradition. He would undoubtedly claim it was better if he was treated for his mental issues in Britain rather than a cell in Cape Town with no date set for the three men's trial.

It was a painful turn of events as all I wanted was to know was what happened. I could not help thinking Anni must have cursed Mngeni from heaven.

The case against Mngeni and Qwabe was, inevitably, put aside. My family and I could only sit and wait for justice to prevail amid all the depression and shock that had inflicted us.

We had to watch the wheels of justice turn slowly in London and now Cape Town as Mngeni's trial was delayed for months to allow him to recover.

Much more was now being revealed about Shrien's alleged homosexuality and I did not know what to make of it all. My son-in-law, while he recovered from his mental health issues, would probably have to explain to his parents why he was regularly being touted as a closet gay.

Certainly I had no evidence that Shrien was gay. I could, perhaps, draw conclusions from his lack of interest in sex with his wife as a possible clue, but that was all.

So I was stunned again to learn that Shrien was said to have been a regular visitor at a gay fetish sex club in London called The Hoist. Naturally, I reached for my laptop as soon as Ashok informed me of the latest rumours in London. The Hoist's website had pictures of semi-naked, shaven-headed men getting close to each other.

Dispatches, the television series my family and I had co-operated with, broadcast Murder on Honeymoon on July 11. It revealed the police had interviewed a man who claimed he had been Shrien's gay lover. The programme also featured claims about The German Master and photographs of him.

Ami had told the Dispatches interviewer that every day she regretted having dismissed Anni's doubts about Shrien as stress. If she hadn't done "maybe she would have been alive today."

I was not having any of that. I was straight on the telephone to reassure her there was nothing anybody could have done to prevent Anni's death except the killers.

Ami was a wonderful sister to Anni and there was no way I was going to let her blame herself. Anni had also talked to me and to Sneha. None of us could have predicted the terrible events that were to follow. It is very easy to blame yourself, I still do that now. But at the same time it is the person who takes another person's life who should be feeling guilt, not the family who truly loved Anni and wanted what was best for her.

Throughout the summer of 2011, Shrien's defence team and doctors argued that his condition was so serious that it would be unsafe to predict when he would be fit to stand trial.

We were back and forth between Sweden and the UK countless times. It was always the same. An alarm clock would go off at 3am and we would be at the airport as the sun rose for the flight from Gothenburg to Stansted, arriving around 10am. Then it was onwards to my sister's home in Harlow or to stay with family in Croydon or Brighton.

We saw less and less of Shrien. After the first few court

appearances he never made it back because the court allowed him to remain in his hospital for treatment.

His counsel, Clare Montgomery the eminent QC, told the judge during one hearing that it would be "positively inhuman" to force Shrien to attend, as he would have to wake at 4am to travel to London from Bristol and then face the return journey.

Ironic really. I did wonder how inhuman it was for my family to suffer as we waited for justice to prevail. Our suffering was permanently written on our faces as we turned out in a large group at hearing after hearing to see when Shrien would be returned to South Africa.

There was even a claim by a senior psychiatrist during one hearing that Shrien could be faking his ill health to avoid being sent to face his accusers. I thought long and hard about this one, discussed it with Ashok, and resolved to say nothing. The doctors needed to decide when he was fit to stand trial.

Shrien had his rights but it would have been fairer on us if the courts had recognised our suffering too. Just the odd mention of how long and how patiently we had been waiting. Some kind of acknowledgement that Anni was my daughter and that I was her grieving father waiting in the wings for the true story and the chance for closure. It's staggering how quickly the actual victim becomes side-lined.

Shrien's legal team were doing their best to keep him in Britain and the result was that the door was repeatedly closed in our faces in terms of allowing us to begin mourning Anni without this major distraction.

When his lawyers went on to claim that South African prosecutors were encouraging claims that Shrien was homosexual, it made me angry. What did it matter to the British courts if he was gay or not? There was a perfectly legitimate extradition agreement between the United Kingdom and South Africa. An extradition order had been lodged and signed and all the legal agreements had been reached. What was happening regarding the evidence against Shrien, or whatever his motivation was for allegedly killing Anni, was an argument for another time and the trial, surely.

I could not understand why the South African case against Shrien was being produced as a reason for not sending him back. He was ill and I accepted that. But after long discussions with my family I decided it best to conceal the growing anger and frustration in me and merely state publicly that I had full faith in the British justice system.

I had chosen the diplomatic path in order not to be seen as desperate and angry at a man who had still to be tried.

People approached me whenever I walked around Belmarsh Magistrates' Court on the many visits we made there, shaking my hand or patting my back, saying they admired my generous spirit and sense of fairness. But inside I was breaking apart and I didn't really know how to handle myself.

After a long day, with all the focus being on Shrien's welfare, the judge finally declared it was strongly in the public interest that the extradition treaty was honoured and that he had complete faith in the South African justice system.

I was overwhelmed, relieved and sobbing, as I heard him say that he would send Shrien back. All it needed was for Home Secretary Theresa May to sanction the decision and Shrien would, at last, be on a plane to Cape Town.

My family were all in tears. We could not really believe that it was, at last, happening and he would go back within, at the most, a few weeks.

Turns out we were right to have such doubts.

Chapter 22

The delay takes its toll

London, England
September, 2011

There were 11,000 reasons to oppose any further delay in extraditing Shrien. My family and friends had organised a quick petition to be presented to the UK Home Office urging Home Secretary Mrs Theresa May to agree to the extradition. Thousands signed in support.

Anni's death had become an internet phenomenon with Facebook pages, Twitter threads and a variety of blogs and discussion groups based on the subject.

We delivered the petition to the Home Office as quickly as we could. I was well aware that Shrien might find another avenue of appeal and I hoped that once the Home Secretary had given the go-ahead it might prove difficult for him to remain in the UK.

Nilam, Ashok, Jayanti and around a dozen family members came with me to hand in the petition which was accepted by a civil servant. If anything it made me feel much better as at least we were doing something constructive with our grief. Our hands had been largely tied as the opposing legal teams went into battle in three courtrooms around London. Each time we hauled ourselves from Sweden, all we could do was sit at the back and listen. But this petition was a positive move for us.

The news we had hoped for was delivered on September 28, 2011. Mrs May agreed that the extradition order was valid and that Shrien should be sent from Britain to Cape Town.

I was back at home in Mariestad when the decision was made public and my phone rang all day with calls from members of the family who wanted to hear it from me, rather than via news programmes, before they could accept it was finally going to happen.

Nilam, as on most other days, moved around our home lighting candles next to Anni's photographs, which had now become permanent fixtures in our front room. She then disappeared into our bedroom to pray. I became a permanent fixture on my phone that day as a variety of callers contacted me to confirm the news directly.

I was warned by Scotland Yard that Shrien still had 14 days in which to appeal the extradition order. I prayed that there should be no such appeal.

Nilam and I didn't think about it. We were determined to stay positive, such was our determination to find out the truth of what happened that night. So we focused on what was to come. We talked about moving to South Africa for the duration of the trial and finding a hotel or a flat where we could stay in Cape Town. It was quite possible that the police would want me as a witness to talk about the troubled engagement. I had also heard that Sneha and The German Master had been interviewed as possible witnesses. Ashok said he was coming too. So were Ami and Anish and several other relations.

But our travel plans were shattered. As Scotland Yard had warned, Shrien gave notice of his plan to appeal against the Home Secretary's order. He applied to the High Court to veto the extradition. None of us knew what would happen next. It felt like every time we made some kind of a progress we'd get some kind of knock back as well. How much more could we take?

I was destroyed by this news once again. Our hopes had been raised by Mrs May and yet Shrien was still not going to get on to that plane. I had run out of things to say to my family and both Nilam and I locked ourselves away for days, trying to understand what was going on. To make some sort of sense of it all.

Shrien had been given all sorts of assurances regarding his health and safety. He would receive special treatment like no other prisoner and kept in a hospital wing in Cape Town. He would sleep alone and be checked regularly by doctors while awaiting trial.

I told Ashok there was nothing more we could do. The South Africans had bent over backwards to help Shrien and would move heaven and earth to protect him. He was their star suspect in a case which had focused attention on them from across the world. If anything happened to him while on South African soil they would forever be held accountable. But Shrien wasn't having any of it. He would not budge and we were back to square one.

Nobody could tell me how long this new appeal would take. It could be days, weeks, months or even years. We were entering another legal black hole with no light.

By now Nilam was mostly bedridden, the sadness filling her eyes at every waking moment. I tried to get on with my work, dealing with any electrical or engineering project that was put my way, but the extradition dodger was a constant burden, weighing me down.

My faith in the British legal system had taken a huge battering and had come crashing down with this latest development in Shrien's favour.

If suffering the blow of the extradition being blocked wasn't enough, Sneha found herself the target of a hateful and anonymous Facebook user who goaded her by saying she could have saved Anni's life.

The writer also knew that we had taken Anni's saris and clothing from Bristol after her death and referred to this in a message ending with the words: "PS. Hope you are comfortable in all your dead cousin's saris that you have taken."

Sneha is an intelligent young woman and she was honest when she told us the Facebook messages had hurt her and made her feel even more guilty about not doing more to stop the marriage.

I asked her father Jayanti to reassure her that nobody in the Hindocha family would ever have a bad word to say about her and we all appreciated the love and affection she'd shown Anni.

But people can be so cruel and this was a striking example of the cowardly and spiteful way people can behave.

Another month passed and Shrien remained in psychiatric care near Bristol. Then November arrived – bringing with it the first anniversary of Anni's murder.

We arranged four candlelight vigils, in London, Bristol, Cape Town and Mariestad. Despite our intense grief that day I was heartened to see they were all well attended.

I sent a video message to well-wishers which was played at the Shree Kadwa Patidar Samaj in Harrow, London. In the video I thanked them for their support and promised that we would get justice for Anni.

Sneha lit candles there, along with other members of the UK-based Hindocha family, spelling out Anni's name.

The vigil in Mariestad was peaceful and all my friends based in Sweden had attended. It was a moment for us where we could show our grief and just say a prayer for Anni. Ami wrote a poem to mark the occasion in which she described her sister as "always shining like a star and having a heart of gold."

I told one interviewer how grateful I was for the support we had received in the year since Anni had left us. I stated that my heart had been broken into a thousand pieces, but everywhere I went I met with good people who helped me pick up a piece each time and put it together again.

But there was a long way to go, both in London and in South Africa. Mngeni and Qwabe were still not ready to face trial because of the former's illness. Christmas came and went with Shrien still holed up in a West Country hospital suffering from various mental health issues.

He was being detained under the Mental Health Act and had been sectioned again for up to six months more.

It was extremely hard for Nilam and me. All we wanted was the full story. All we were getting was how important Shrien's health was to one and all. My wife's health was failing by the day. Her weakness was causing me great concern as she still had issues with her cancer. The UK courts just had to help and give us the strength to carry on.

It was widely claimed in the courts that it would have been "unjust" to send Shrien back at this stage. To me it seemed that order signed by the Home Secretary was worth no more than the paper it was written on.

I was all for a fair and balanced court system but where was the fairness towards me?

There were top class medical facilities in Cape Town. After all, it was where Dr. Christiaan Barnard had performed the world's first heart transplant and the city had a top ranking hospital in his name. Cape Town was a civilised place and the standards of hospital care were as good as anywhere. But still Shrien wasn't going back and I was not sure I could take another six months of waiting.

My brothers were brilliant in helping me hold it together and it was always comforting to have Ami and Anish by my side. Holding our two grandchildren also gave Nilam and me a wonderful boost. Somehow we managed to make it through Christmas and the harsh winter that followed.

The BBC broadcast a Panorama special on Anni's murder the night before we were due to hear in the High Court whether Shrien was at last going back. The producers had CCTV footage of Shrien passing a package to Tongo at the Cape Grace Hotel and introduced the possibility that he may have been thinking of taking Anni on a surprise helicopter trip, which was the first anybody in my family had heard of it. Why had he never mention anything about a helicopter trip to me in South Africa or in any of our family meetings? I wondered why he had never mentioned it to anyone in the Hindocha family before.

I found the programme largely speculative, raising many questions but delivering very few answers. The answers had to come from the court in Cape Town, but the BBC did raise awareness of Anni's murder once again, as the public's interest in the case had understandably died down over the previous few months. So the next day the High Court in London was packed and the Hindochas were crammed into two rows of seats right alongside the Dewanis. We watched our words very carefully.

Once again Shrien was the winner as two judges ruled he could remain in Britain and should be extradited only once he was fully fit.

The judges, Sir John Thomas and Mr Justice Ouseley, agreed that the case could be sent back to Judge Riddle for a fresh look at the medical evidence on Shrien.

Around 20 members of the Hindocha family were there in the High Court to be kicked in the teeth once more. The misery was palpable. I looked at Nilam and my legs almost buckled as we came down the marble hallways and descended the stairs in the dejected routine we had become accustomed to.

My agitation was such that Ashok stopped me from speaking to the phalanx of television cameras, reporters and photographers who had gathered outside. He was concerned that I might utter a few choice phrases about the British legal system or end up saying something which might harm the case against Shrien.

Ashok was right to hold me back. I could not control my

rage easily that day. I was shaking and trying my level best not to reveal the torment going on inside me, particularly as Shrien's family were all around us.

It was left to dear Ami to deliver some very measured words about wanting Shrien to get better quickly and be well enough to travel.

It was now the end of March 2012 and almost a year and a half since Anni died yet I still felt we were nowhere nearer discovering the truth and getting closure. Anni would have been 30 this month. So young. On her birthday we went to Lake Vänern and lit some candles for her. It was nice to say a prayer and feel that although she was gone, at least she was close to us.

Losing Anni was terrible but this relentless pursuit of truth and justice was just so unfair on us. Nilam and I were traumatised by the refusal to send Shrien back and Ashok correctly stated that we were now "living like zombies."

Shrien's family issued a statement saying they were grateful that he was being allowed to stay and that he was innocent but determined to clear his name and to "seek justice for Anni."

That made my blood boil even further. If Shrien really wanted to seek justice for Anni he should man up and get his backside over to Cape Town without any further hesitation.

Sadly, waiting was to be a big part of our lives for a very long and painful time to come.

Chapter 23

Three down, one to go?

London, England
July, 2012

It was to be a long, long wait for justice. With Shrien using every tactic to prevent his return, we had to look to the South Africans to set an example for the British courts.

I had already sanctioned the plea bargain of Zola Tongo, as was my right under the South African legal system. I had consulted Ashok and Jayanti to hear their views before signing his jail term document. We agreed that seven years off a normal 25 year sentence wasn't that much of a reduction in return for turning state witness.

So I cannot overemphasise the pain I was in when we reached the end of July and Shrien was still biding his time and avoiding his accusers. We learned that he was allowed home visits several hours per day and enjoyed daily workouts in his parents swimming pool and gym. He was also allowed to use a laptop and was now spending time in a caravan in the hospital grounds. If it wasn't so devastating it would have been bizarre.

Things were to get worse when we attended the High Court in London on July 30, 2012, more than eighteen months since

Anni's murder. The London Olympics had begun and the city had been transformed into one big celebration. Everywhere we went, people were suddenly more polite, helpful and smiling. But there was little reason for us to be as joyful.

Shrien's legal team told Judge Riddle that keeping him under his current medical regime for 12 more months would speed up his recovery. I could not believe what was being asked. Another whole year. Who did he think he was? The King of England?

Apparently Shrien was making a recovery, albeit a slow one, and his anxiety about the court proceedings was stalling his healing. How ridiculous. I was so dismayed and could not believe what I was hearing. It just felt as if he was now playing the system to the maximum. It seemed like he didn't want to go back. Maybe we would never know the whole story of that night.

Justice Riddle was not buying it that easily and agreed that a psychiatrist engaged by the South Africans should examine Shrien to provide more information about his condition. So we were off again, this time until September 18.

Thankfully the courts in Cape Town were not so slow. A week after the debacle in the London High Court, Qwabe's trial was drawing to a close.

I travelled to Cape Town at this time. I discovered that some insensitive people there had produced T-shirts with the logo "Dewani Tours" in Hindi-style writing. And a further message on them said: "Treat Your Wife to a Killer Holiday." This callous cashing-in on the murder of my daughter was not in the least bit funny and not appreciated by me.

I was in Cape Town for a reason. The trial of Xolile

Mngeni was ongoing and I wanted to get some more information about what had happened to Anni. This was the last person who had seen Anni alive. My adorable niece Nishma accompanied me. I put my arm around her shoulders as she broke down in tears when details of how Anni was murdered were given.

Qwabe admitted his part in killing Anni and therefore saved a lot of court time. But the most striking part of the proceedings, as far as I was concerned, was the fact that he claimed Tongo had hired him and Mngeni on behalf of Shrien to kill his wife. Qwabe was to be paid £1,100 by Tongo. That was his price for my daughter's life. I would have raised £100 million or more for him if he had talked to me first before taking her life.

Qwabe was put away for 25 years for murdering my daughter, as well as for kidnapping and robbery.

So that meant two murderers down with two more men still to be tried. But both were suffering illness which was preventing them from standing trial.

I had heard that Mngeni's prognosis had not been good and that he was genuinely very ill. At one stage it was touch and go whether he would live, such were the complications in treating his brain tumour.

I believe I am a compassionate man who naturally sees the good in people and wishes only the best for all. But it would be far from the truth if I said I felt any sympathy for Mngeni. I wanted him to live only because whatever he told the court under cross-examination would help provide more information on how Anni died.

Mngeni was accused of firing the gun that took Anni's

life. With that pulling of the trigger he had ended Anni's life and plunged me and my family into a living hell. I challenge fathers everywhere to say they would not have shared my extreme feelings.

Mngeni had admitted shooting Anni and then retracted his admission of guilt. This was a cruel toying with my emotions. He had three children and for those I could feel sorry. But did he care for my child as he put a gun to her neck and took her life? Not one iota. This was a ruthless criminal who had been accused of killing another man six years earlier.

I wanted my pound of flesh. Tongo down. Qwabe down. Now only Mngeni to be caged forever and the whole mystery of Shrien to be solved.

A few days after Qwabe was jailed for 25 years, Mngeni appeared in court and I agreed to testify and tell the court what I knew. I was also asked to identify Anni's Nokia phone, a BlackBerry and her watch. All had been recovered from the hitmen.

Addressing the court was an ordeal I knew I had to endure for the sake of the truth and for Anni.

Mngeni was a skinny rake and walked into the court with the aid of a walking stick. I still did not feel at all sorry for him. He was virtually penniless. The prosecutor, Adrian Mopp, told me he was unsure how Mngeni had been able to afford a privately funded lawyer.

As I took the stand a dispute broke out between the defence and prosecution after I was asked by Mngeni's lawyer, Matthews Dayimani, whether I approved of Anni's marriage to Shrien.

It was an odd question for him to ask on behalf of Mngeni

and I believed it had nothing to do with the man sitting in the dock.

Judge Robert Henney allowed the question after Mr Dayimani said it was linked to allegations that Anni was killed in a conspiracy.

I was not sure where he was going with his line of questioning, but I responded truthfully when I said: "I approved of the marriage, yes. Why should I not?"

There was a further dispute when the lawyer asked me if I had paid for the wedding.

Mr Mopp jumped to his feet and accused Dayimani of going on a fishing expedition, adding that Mngeni was not paying for his services and that his role in the trial was "questionable."

Later, Mr Dayimani told reporters outside that his fees were not being met by Shrien Dewani's family but by human rights activists from Kenya, one of whom was called Mr Edmondo.

It puzzled the prosecutors and me how Mngeni had been able to hire such a top-flight lawyer and I took that burning question with me as I flew back to London as soon as I had completed my evidence. I still have no idea who this person Mr Edmondo was and how he came to play an influential part in the trial.

I just hoped the South Africans would conduct a fair and proper trial of Mngeni and then put him away for a long time. But I was still more keen to know whether Shrien had played any part in the murder of my daughter or not.

Unsurprisingly, we faced another delay when we returned to court in London in September. Medical reports were not ready. Another month's delay, despite Judge Riddle being told that Shrien's condition had improved.

I was not holding my breath as my family and I wheeled our suitcases out of the court before heading for the airport and home. It had been such a short hearing. We gathered in a Pizza Express restaurant on Baker Street for an early lunch and agreed that there was to be no mention of Shrien as we all ate.

The October court date arrived. Once again we headed back home to Sweden – still none the wiser after yet another adjournment and facing another hefty credit card bill for flights.

The second anniversary of Anni's journey to heaven came and went. November 13 also coincided with the Hindu Diwali festival which is normally celebrated with huge fanfare. This time though we marked it with private prayers. There were no traditional lights to mark Diwali in my home, only darkness.

Ashok and I sat down and wondered when God would put an end to our misery and give us closure. We agreed that two years was a long time to wait for a man to make a simple plane journey. My concern was for Nilam and the rest of the family. We had lost Anni and suffered two years of being ignored by the courts in Britain, who only had ears for Shrien's welfare.

My pain was eased by the fact that two men had gone to jail and the third was before the judge in Cape Town. There was progress being made but Shrien still had to go back and I looked forward to the next UK hearing on December 2 for him to be ordered back to Cape Town.

Mngeni was declared to have murdered Anni when the judge delivered his verdict on November 19 and confirmed that he was the man who shot Anni. He had claimed he had made his initial admission while being tortured by police who had placed a plastic bag over his head and threatened to suffocate him. My worries were eased by the fact that he had been given a fair trial and had been able to present his defence, allowing the judge to make his decision after hearing all the evidence against him and assessing it properly.

I still didn't know who funded his defence costs and neither did the South African prosecutors or police. But I had been pretty confident he was responsible for shooting Anni. The police had reassured me for two years that they had got the right man as his DNA and palm print had been found on Tongo's taxi. There was no doubt he was there and he took Anni's life.

Mngeni and Qwabe had accused each other of firing the single shot that killed Anni. As far as I was concerned they were both evil. The judge even mentioned in his verdict that Mngeni was a "merciless and evil person" who deserved the maximum sentence. He had shown no remorse whatsoever.

It would be sad for their families, especially their large number of children, who would be directly punished by their fathers being locked away, but that was the way it had to be.

The law had to do its job and act as a deterrent to others who might think about taking a precious life so callously. There are many, many murders each year in South Africa and the police go about their business in such dangerous conditions. The courts have to impose tough sentences and support the diligent police work. There can be no nonsense from the courts, otherwise parts of South Africa could easily become like the Wild West with so many guns in the hands of stony-hearted individuals and gangs.

I did not feel so angry with Tongo. The more I learned, the more I came to feel he was a stupid man who had ruined his own life by getting involved in a murder plot which was completely out of character. He had five children and had worked hard to feed them by driving taxis and putting in long hours.

He had seven years taken off his tariff with my agreement. I had been able to show him some compassion for his absurd flirtation with Cape Town's criminal world. Although nothing was going to bring Anni back, justice was being served.

Three had gone down – now it remained only for Shrien to face his accusers and for the truth to come out.

Chapter 24

Why was Shrien still in the UK?

London, England
December, 2012

I could see that the South Africans were getting as fed up as I was with the delays from the UK courts regarding Shrien's extradition.

There had been much consternation in South Africa over why Shrien had not resurfaced there. Politicians, academics, journalists and even comedians had piled into the argument. The women of the African National Congress began a campaign to demand the swift return of Shrien. It was a positive move. Any help I could receive in putting pressure on the London courts was welcome.

My voice was hardly being heard at all. I lived in a permanent state of disbelief that two years had passed with the main suspect still remaining in Britain.

Whenever I sat down with my family to privately discuss Shrien's intransigence, I would blame myself for not preventing him from leaving South Africa so quickly after Anni's death.

I had signed the medical papers and documents to release her body shortly after arriving in Cape Town. My family reminded me, though, that at that point Shrien was not a suspect. At the time I had been desperate to leave with Anni – to bring her home and away from the place where she had died.

A few days more and the police would have made a move on Shrien and stopped him from flying out, meaning this impasse would have been avoided. Shrien could have answered their questions there and then and the law might have taken its course. It would probably have been all over within a year.

Instead, two years on and with a massive deterioration in my health and hundreds and hundreds of sleepless nights, we were all still waiting.

The courts had once again given us hope that Shrien's plane ticket would be booked on December 3 at the next hearing. Nilam, Anish and Ashok accompanied me on the flight from Gothenburg to Stansted and down the M11 to London. It was to be the first leg of the journey for Anish and me, as we would be heading directly to Cape Town after the proceedings at Westminster Magistrates' Court.

I was distraught once again to sit in court and hear that Shrien was still not fit to travel. I told Ashok that Shrien could have travelled in comfort with Anish and me, as we would have looked after him on the flight to Cape Town and ensured his safe arrival.

This time the judge gave Shrien six more months to get himself over his depression and post-traumatic stress.

There was no ruler available to measure how long such an ailment can inflict a person. I had no idea at all. But I still

wondered why he couldn't be sent to South Africa
immediately and be treated there.

Outside I found myself telling the media that six months
was another long period to wait. I told them I still had faith
in the legal system but inside I was struggling to maintain my
dignity and control my anger.

Like many times before, we wheeled our suitcases from the
court and into taxis. The family left for Mariestad, Anish and
I for South Africa.

Cape Town gave us a very different picture as Mngeni
was sent down for life – the judge branding him as callous,
merciless, evil and brutal. He looked like an innocent
schoolboy in his purple cardigan and white baseball cap. But
when he trudged gingerly away on his Zimmer frame, he
looked every inch the old man he was destined to become in
jail. His life, at 23, was wasted too.

I hadn't planned to talk to the media but outside the court
Anish and I were swamped by the cameras. I spoke from the
heart: "I have come here straight from London, where Shrien
Dewani's case about coming to South Africa was being heard.

"I wanted to look into Mngeni's eyes – the eyes of the man
who murdered my daughter – and ask him why?

"But he would not look at me. He is a spineless and weak
coward. With Mngeni being jailed today, it means three
people out of five in that car have been sentenced.

"But the story of why my beautiful, innocent and loving
Anni was shot dead here in your city remains incomplete.

"The full picture will only emerge once Shrien Dewani is
back here in Cape Town to face trial.

"He is ill, suffering from post-traumatic stress. But what about us?

"My wife Nilam and I have never slept a full night since Anni was taken from us, and Shrien holds the key. He must come back here as soon as possible and I pray that it is not too long.

"Anni is never coming back, we know that for sure, and we grieve as a family each minute, each hour and each week as the time passes by.

"But we need all the questions answered so we can move on with our lives. It is going to be hard without Anni, but I will keep on fighting with the support of you all and bring Shrien here to face the many questions he needs to answer, and close this case.

"I am heartened by the support we have received from the many, many thousands of good South Africans who have supported us and I feel ashamed that Anni was killed here on your streets while she was on her honeymoon.

"I look forward to coming back in the not too distant future to see Shrien Dewani face trial and receive full closure on this terrible episode in my life."

Christmas came and passed once again. We did our best to make it a merry one for our grandchildren who came to visit from Stockholm with Ami and her husband Henning, who had been a pillar of support to his wife and to us all.

He understood the anxieties of Ami and her need to be at the London courts whenever possible. He was always there to take care of their children without any fuss when she travelled to the UK.

WRONG TURN LED TO BRIDE MURDER

▶ Carjacking cabbie got lost
▶ Widower joins killer hunt

Above: Shrien and Anni stayed at the luxurious Cape Grace Hotel for their honeymoon.

Right: Daily Mirror. November 15, 2010.

Left: Daily Mirror. November 16, 2010.

BRIT BRIDE KILLED BY CARJACKERS

Body is found on back seat

A BRITISH wife has been murdered on her honeymoon in South Africa when she and her husband were carjacked.

Above: Police in Gugulethu. Anni's body was discovered in the back of the taxi.

© Getty Images

TAKE THE RINGS.. BUT LET HER LIVE
Man's arrested over South Africa bride killing

By RICHARD SMITH
richard.smith@mirror.co.uk

DESPERATE husband Shrien Dewani begged carjackers to take their expensive rings and cash to spare his wife's life, it emerged yesterday.

The millionaire businessman was honeymooning with bride Anni, 28, in South Africa when gunmen hijacked their cab and killed her with three shots at point blank range.

Police revealed yesterday that a 26-year-old man has been arrested in connection with the shooting.

Thirty-year-old Shrien's

plan was revealed by brother Preyen, who said: "Shrien offered them wedding and engagement rings, their watches, cash and mobile phones.

"The robbers took these items, then told Shrien to leave the vehicle. He refused, and after a struggle, they pushed him out as it was driving along."

Anni was later found dead in the cab near Cape Town on Saturday.

Preyen, 32, added: "Anni was incredibly beautiful, a smiling, bubbly personality. They were excited, like any couple going on honeymoon."

The brothers are directors of £15million care home firm PSP Healthcare.

The couple married in Mumbai and flew home to Westbury-on-Trym, Bristol, to celebrate the Hindu festival of Diwali, then left for South Africa last Tuesday and were four days into their honeymoon when tragedy struck.

Anni's body will be flown back to Britain later this week for a funeral and memorial service.

Anni was incredibly beautiful, with a smiling, bubbly personality

▲ SO HAPPY The couple were excited about life

Left: Daily Mirror. November 17, 2010.

Below: Xolile Mngeni from Khayelitsha was charged with Anni's murder – just three days after her body was found. He was later convicted of firing the shot that killed Anni and sentenced to life.

Above: The immigration authorities presented Anni's passport to me before we left South Africa to return to the UK with Anni's body. They'd stamped DECEASED on the same page as her entry stamp at O.R. Tambo Airport, Johannesburg, just nine days earlier.

Right: Daily Mirror. November 18, 2010.

CHARGED
Honeymoon carjack: Man accused of bride murder

By ANDREW GREGORY
andrew.gregory@mirror.co.uk

A MAN has been charged with the murder of honeymoon bride Anni Dewani in South Africa, police said last night.

Anni, 28, and millionaire husband Shrien, 30, were attacked by armed carjackers on the outskirts of Cape Town on Saturday night.

They forced Shrien and the driver out before speeding off. Her body was found the next day.

Police confirmed a 26-year-old man from the township of Khayelitsha will appear in court today charged with murder and hijacking.

Mr Dewani, of Westbury-on-Trym, Bristol, said: "It's good news. The police are very positive they

have the right guy. They have told me that all the elements match: forensics, accent, background and alibi."

A post-mortem examination showed Mrs Dewani, who grew up in Sweden, died from a single gunshot wound to the neck. There is no indication she was sexually assaulted.

Her body has now been released to her family and is expected to be flown back to Britain later this week for a funeral and memorial service.

The Dewanis, who'd only been married a fortnight, had decided to venture outside the normal tourist areas for a more authentic experience.

Mr Dewani, a director of a £15million care home firm, said: "She had never been to Africa before, so she suggested that we should have a look at the 'real Africa'."

▲ TARGET Police recover the car

BIG DAY Couple wed in Mumbai

They've told me all elements match: background, accent, alibi SHRIEN ON ARREST

Above: Shrien was arrested on December 8, 2010, at the request of the South African authorities.

Above: Mziwamadoda Qwabe. *Top:* Zola Tongo.

Daily Mirror. December 8, 2010.

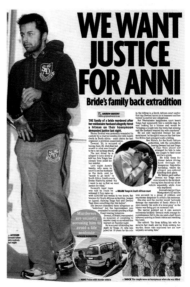

Daily Mirror. December 9, 2010.

Above: Shrien leaves Southmead Police Station in Bristol flanked by police officers after fulfilling conditions of his bail.

Above: Sneha lights a candle in honour of her beloved cousin at the Shree Kadwa Patidar Samaj in Harrow – one year after her murder.

Above: Our family arriving at Westminster Magistrates Court, London, for the extradition hearing.

Above: Ashok, on the left, and Anish at a press conference in London.

Above: Nilam and me at the High Court in London for the extradition hearing.

Above: Anish, Nilam, Ami and me at yet another court hearing.

Above: Shrien arrives at Western Cape Crown Court in South Africa on October 6, 2014 – almost four years after Anni's death. *Below:* I am met by a media frenzy.

Above: I catch up with the local news on the balcony of our apartment.

Above: The evidence is laid out in court. It's hard to look at Anni's belongings.

Above: Our family stuck together throughout the trial. We are very close to one another.

Shrien in court. He did not look at me once.

Above: CCTV footage from the Cape Grace Hotel on November 16, 2010, was shown in court. You can see Shrien, Tongo and even me in the images.

Above: Anish told the media it would be a "terrible development" if the trial ended.

Above: Judge Jeanette Traverso who presided over the case.

Above: We laid 32 roses at the spot where Anni died as this was the age she would have been if she had lived. *Below left:* A visit to Kruger park where Anni went on safari before Cape Town. *Below right:* On Nilam's birthday, she noticed the word 'Anni' on a bottle in the exact same handwriting that Anni used. She felt it was a sign from her.

Above: We were left shattered after the verdict but went out the front door with our heads held high in spite of the series of blows we had suffered as a family.
Below: Anni's ashes were scattered at Lake Vänern close to our home in Mariestad.

The delay in Shrien going back to face police questioning showed no sign of easing when, in February, we learned that his family had issued a statement saying he had suffered chest pains and that his health had seriously deteriorated. Apparently, Shrien had suffered a poor reaction to the medication he had been prescribed to improve his mental health.

Two dates in April and the first day of July had been set aside for Shrien's case to be reviewed in London. I did not need a crystal ball to see what was going to happen next. His mental health issues had now been combined with a breakdown in his physical state.

I told the family we had to prepare ourselves for another year of mental hardship too. When I was alone, I could not help cursing the day he entered my life.

It appeared that Shrien was evidently going to cause as much disruption as possible to obstruct his path to justice. I knew I had to be strong. I had to find some way of getting through this prolonged agony. Everywhere I looked within the Hindocha nearest and dearest I saw their agony too. The youngsters were quite adept at shielding their sadness and I suppose that youthful zest was a natural way to mask the tears.

Jayanti's youngest daughter Nira, one of the few Hindocha youngsters left in Mariestad, was ploughing along with her career as a disc jockey. She and I would regularly sit and chat about Anni, ending up in laughter or tears, wherever the memories took us.

Meanwhile, Ashok bought the Stadt Hotel in the centre

of the town. I was pleased as this would give him a good
diversion during the wait for justice. He had been incredibly
supportive and loving throughout this awful ordeal and I
worried about his own health. He was being the strong one
for us all, always there to deal with the police, media and
other inquiries whenever needed. He is 11 years younger and
is very respectful towards both Jayanti and me, and as faithful
as a brother can be. He has been a powerful means for us to
keep Anni's name in the spotlight and stop all the focus being
totally on Shrien.

The acquisition of the Stadt Hotel gave Ashok new focus
and meant that his wife Nisha and Jayanti could be involved
and make it a family business. Both help out with the food
preparation and other duties such as supervising cleaning
and reception work. I was pleased that Nira became the
hotel's house DJ. Her Saturday night parties are full of the
youngsters from the area who swarm to the club there for a
weekly dance. Nira is a highly skilled DJ, but on the few
occasions I have happened to be in the hotel when she is
spinning the discs the music has been far too loud for these
old ears.

I even began to find a way of getting involved in the
hotel myself, taking charge of the wiring and any electricity
problems, including fixing the controls to the lift buttons when
they have been out of order. Anything to distract me.

Nilam and I often pop into the hotel restaurant for the
excellent buffet lunch Ashok serves up. It is always busy and
we tend to eat with Ashok, Nisha and Jayanti after the large
number of diners have departed so that we can enjoy some

peace and quiet. There is always the London courts to talk about.

If I don't feel like eating there, Nilam is an excellent cook and I often help her in the kitchen. Ba, of course, is the master chef of the family and she has been known to get cross if her three sons do not eat lunch at her table at least once a week.

The weeks and months went by and winter soon took its hold. All the family cars were fitted with snow gripping tyres for the season, which are essential if one is to keep a vehicle from getting stuck or slipping across the lanes. Normal chores, in an unreal existence.

April saw the return of Shrien's extradition battle at the Westminster Court and although the hearing was told his condition was improving, I wasn't convinced.

To all intents and purposes, the court was informed he could be ready to go to South Africa in three months. He was no longer suicidal and his depression had eased. But he was still experiencing post-traumatic stress and doctors could not be one hundred percent sure that he would not self-harm. The doubts, therefore, were still there.

We had been here time and time again. I walked towards Baker Street underground station followed by the family, seething at what we had just heard.

July came along and this latest hearing was set for five days. I could not understand why the situation could not be sorted in five hours.

More than two and a half years had passed since Anni's murder. Three men had been jailed. There had been countless court hearings. We had been back and forth, back and forth. Surely it wasn't necessary to go over all the old stuff once more.

All we wanted to know was if Shrien was now ready to face justice. A simple yes or no from the judge was all that was required. Everybody had had more than their say. I wished the judge would just make a quick ruling.

Instead, it was a torturous five days that ensued.

Mr Hugo Keith QC represented the South African government. He was clearly a highly competent lawyer and he got used to seeing the large Hindocha family gathered at each hearing.

I also sensed he appreciated that English was the third language for some of us and therefore we didn't fully comprehend the legal terms uttered in court. In private briefings for us afterwards he always politely explained in the simplest terms what it all meant.

He told the court that there had been positive signs from Shrien that he was recovering and that he would receive top level medical care once he reached South Africa.

But a drawback came in the evidence presented by a psychiatrist who argued if Shrien was sent back he would have "to deal with the events that formed his nightmares." This effectively meant that reality would be too much for Shrien and that was enough reason to keep him in Britain.

I thought it was a limp defence but my experience of the UK legal system and its keenness to protect the rights of suspects made me believe that Shrien would once again win the day.

We were told to come back on July 24 to hear the decision. I was not going to hold my breath. There was no way Shrien was going to be returning to South Africa after all the sympathy that had gone his way.

July 24 arrived, a Wednesday. There was the biggest number of Hindochas I had seen in court thus far, all prepared for the usual announcement of yet another delay.

None of us could believe it when Judge Riddle agreed that Shrien should be extradited. At last.

Chapter 25

We just want answers

London, England
October, 2013

It did not take long for Shrien to try to avoid getting on that plane. We had been told to expect he would be on his way within a few weeks. That was not to be the case.

He appealed to the courts again, claiming he was still unfit and he needed to be certain that his health and safety were assured in South Africa. This time, to be successful, his objection had to be related to a point of law. And successful he was.

On October 22, three judges at the Royal Courts of Justice decided that there were still legal issues to be resolved over the extradition.

The judges questioned whether it might be "unjust and oppressive" to send Shrien back while his health issues were still not cleared up.

If it hadn't been for nearly three years of such nonsensical delays I would not have believed it. I was raw with anger at how this could be allowed to happen again. Might Shrien still be in his comfortable caravan, surfing the web and enjoying time with his family, long after I had gone?

There were tears from Nilam. She had generally kept in the background as far as speaking publicly, granting only a few interviews.

This time she rounded on the media and told them: "I am the mother of a murdered daughter. How long do I have to wait?"

It was a perfectly reasonable question. As we made our way back to Stansted and on to Mariestad, we stopped at a Hindu temple in East London to pray for Anni and ask God for the answers. Somebody had to tell us when we would discover the truth, receive justice and reach the end of this terrible episode of waiting.

I wanted our lives to function again. I wanted to be able to begin mourning Anni properly once the whole affair had been cleared up. Her soul needed to rest in peace as well, and as her father I had to fight as hard as I could for justice.

But things were more desperate than they had ever been. The third anniversary of Anni's death was approaching and we had been given another extension to our sentence.

I sat on the Ryanair jet later that night, unable to speak even to Nilam. I was numbed by the lack of consideration being shown to my wife and my family by the British courts. I had insisted repeatedly that I had the utmost faith in the British people and their legal system. We had received many thousands of letters and messages of support from Britain and from around the globe leading me to proclaim Anni as a "daughter of the world."

The courts in the UK had been advocates of balance and human rights. But now scant regard was being shown to my human rights. In fact it was absolutely inhumane to treat us this way.

Anni had been taken from us in such a cruel manner yet we were no nearer reaching the closure that would allow us to move into private and proper mourning.

It was not just us who were waiting for an end, but millions of people who had been following developments on their front pages, television screens or on social media and the internet.

I knew I had to keep a protective eye on my family, particularly my wife.

Nilam had lost weight and hardly ate. Her strength was being reduced each day. She had stopped her daily walks and spent days on end lying in bed, trying to sleep off the horror of it all.

She is a very bright woman and I am sure some might interpret her preference to remain silent most of the time as a sign that she had no voice. But her pain spoke volumes. I was so weary of seeing her crying through the night, wailing for Anni and then for some sort of relief.

This was a woman who had been through cancer. Now the daughter who had put her life on hold for a year to care for her had gone. Neither Nilam nor I knew where to turn or who to turn to. Our faith in justice was being destroyed each time the courts held a hearing into Shrien's situation.

We had always been a secure and loving family unit. That had been destroyed on the night Shrien took Anni into a dangerous township. We just wanted answers from him.

Guilty or innocent, it actually didn't matter much to us at that stage. We just wanted him to tell us all what really happened and for the proceedings to end. We hadn't even reached the stage of exploring the inconsistencies in the different versions he had given to various people. That was for the trial, the prosecutors and the defence to argue about.

But in London the soul-destroying delay seemed endless. Perhaps Great Britain needs to introduce a law that sets a limit on the time an extradition order has to be carried out, once it has been served, so that suspects are forced on to a plane if it can be shown that the same standard of care is available at the destination.

Travelling from London Heathrow to Cape Town involves a flight of around 12 hours. When you think the legal tussle had been going on for three years, a flight of that length would not seem that difficult. Shrien could board a flight at 8pm, have dinner, sleep for eight hours and be ready to wake up in Cape Town.

Shrien was mentally ill. But the South Africans had done everything possible to ensure the best medical attention and facilities for him. I was pretty sure that once he had arrived there and been handed to medical experts, it would not take another three years to see him fit to stand trial.

I just would have liked the opportunity to address the London courts personally, as the father of the victim.

As there was nothing I could do regarding the extradition proceedings, I had to turn to the media to funnel my messages. Not all the media were helpful, however. I took issue with the BBC Panorama programme 'The Honeymoon Murder: Who Killed Anni?' which I found insensitive and badly timed, only contributing to our stress. The BBC rejected my protests saying the programme had been broadcast to "test the factual evidence."

I would have thought that task would be best left to a judge in Cape Town.

In fact my nephew Amit wrote to the Leveson Inquiry suggesting an independent media advisor or consultant should be assigned to every family involved in high-profile cases.

Amit, who like all the other cousins was extremely close to Anni, told Lord Justice Leveson in his letter that, on the first day of the extradition proceedings at Westminster, the hearing was in the same place as the Julian Assange extradition case, in the same court room and in front of the same judge.

Amit stated that there was a large number of journalists covering both cases and that our encounters with them were "ferocious and aggressive, almost like lambs to the slaughter."

Amit added: "Nothing can prepare you for fifty plus press vying for your picture and comments or statement."

It was a clever idea and although his lengthy plea was too late to be considered by Leveson's inquiry, I do hope that the British government does its best to help families like us who sadly find themselves in similar situations.

To be clear, I am not talking about the familiar family liaison officers, who do a great job, but properly trained and independent media experts who are not tied to the press or the courts.

I understand the media have a job to do. But I had never come across such a frenzy before. Anni's beautiful face helped sell newspapers and I came to terms with that. TV audience figures went up when her image was transmitted and that was why news bulletins regularly opened with Anni's murder.

Her death was sensational, involving beauty, money, horrible violence, and sexual claim and counter-claim. There were enough characters involved in the case to help produce a hit thriller. I got that. But I was wholly unprepared for the level of interest.

That said, I was proud that the world recognised my daughter's beauty, the perfect riposte to Shrien's rejection of her which made her feel ugly.

I must also add that the majority of the press had been very fair with us and saw us as exactly what we were, a family lost and in grief. Their questions were mostly sensitive and respectful and I will always owe a huge debt to Ashok for his rapid development of skills in media diplomacy and understanding how best to handle their demands.

It went largely quiet again over Christmas and we hoped and prayed that at the next hearing Shrien would finally be on his way.

We were due back in court on Friday, January 31. Despite everything, I still hadn't given up hope. But the prospect of yet another needless journey to London in such harsh winter weather prevented us from making the date.

I was certain that the judges would decide to keep him longer in Britain and we would only have to make the same journey back in utter dejection. More importantly, Nilam had been in hospital and her health was failing. She had been advised not to travel.

To our complete surprise, the judges threw out Shrien's appeal and upheld Judge Riddle's decision. There were only a handful of Hindochas who had bothered to attend, clearly fearing a repeat of the same adjournment nonsense. So it was left to Amit to deliver our reaction to the TV cameras and I was proud of him as I watched the news that night.

It had been three years since Judge Riddle had originally

ordered Shrien to be extradited. Shrien could make one final attempt in early March at the High Court but he was as good as on his way when an application to appeal to the Supreme Court was turned down.

The High Court refused him any further appeals and he was told he had 28 days to leave the country and comply with his extradition order. He had exhausted every avenue of appeal and probably exhausted every member of my family.

His D-Day was staring him in the face. All the love and encouragement he had received from his family, supporters and professional representatives had been useful in staying his extradition – but now it was time for him to finally face his accusers and tell us the whole truth and nothing but the truth. To give us closure and proper respect to his late wife.

This REALLY was it.

Chapter 26

The wait is over. Almost

Mariestad, Sweden
March, 2014

The mood within the Hindocha households around
Europe, particularly in Mariestad, was lifted. A large
grey cloud had passed over us and a ray of light had finally
shone through. There were no celebrations. There couldn't
be. We had lost our irreplaceable Anni. Nothing was going to
change that or bring her back. But I noticed things became
calmer and some of the smiles returned to our faces.

It had been a long three and a half year wait. A wretched
time for us. There had been upset after upset, endless tears,
and the suffering, torment and pain my wonderful family had
endured amounted to nothing short of persecution.

All we had ever asked for was the truth. The one person
who could help us had remained 6,000 miles away from his
accusers for all that time. Now the wait was over.

Rodney de Kock and Adrian Mopp, the prosecutors, were
on the phone regularly from Cape Town giving us updates on
arrangements for Shrien in South Africa.

He had spent the past 18 months living in a camper van in
the grounds of the Blaise View centre near Bristol. He had

also been allowed to visit his family daily.

In South Africa, Shrien was to be held in the Valkenberg psychiatric hospital and given a private room, which had been redecorated for his arrival. It was to be in Ward 4 and there would be 24-hour observation because of his reported suicidal tendencies.

If he wished he would be able to pay for his own chef to prepare his meals and, along with the other patients on the general ward, Shrien would be offered group therapy, belly-dancing classes plus sewing and cookery tuition. If he wanted to visit a beauty salon and a barber, that would be sanctioned too.

Actually I wasn't too bothered about the minutiae of Shrien's stay in Cape Town and how comfortable they'd made it for him. But the facts were widely reported and unavoidable.

At the end of the day, the South Africans had to do everything humanly possible to ensure Shrien was fit and ready for the trial. If that meant pampering him like a king then it could only be a good thing.

We could not have waited much longer for the trial to begin. Absolutely nothing was worth risking a setback in his recovery.

In my imagination I was just fast-forwarding to the moment he would finally appear in court to answer our questions. I couldn't help it and neither could Nilam. My sense of relief at the fact that he was going to South Africa at last was immense. But new anxieties were beginning to kick in.

Now I worried about the length of time it had taken to bring him to the Cape Town court and whether the witnesses would be able to remember everything. Indeed, would Shrien have a memory which was a hundred percent reliable? Would any of us after all that time?

What terrible new details of Anni's last minutes of life would we have to listen to? Much as we wanted the truth, we had to be prepared to hear some horrendous details. And what was the outcome going to be? Nilam and I were very worried.

The prosecutors asked if I would give my permission or approval to appeals from the world's broadcasters to be allowed to broadcast the trial live.

South Africa had just experienced its first live transmission of a major court case as Oscar Pistorius went on trial, accused of murdering his girlfriend Reeva Steenkamp.

It had made for riveting television, attracting viewers in massive numbers. I had already approved of Anni being declared a "daughter of the world" because I knew interest in her and sympathy over her death had been global.

I was in favour of the idea of television showing the trial. My family and others supported my wish and I gave the go-ahead to the South Africans. But I believe the defendant's team did not want it to be televised and the final decision would rest with the judge.

On a practical level it was difficult for Nilam and me to know when to head for South Africa. We were told Shrien would leave on April 7, appear before the court and then be sent to the prison hospital to continue his rehabilitation.

But I was also warned that the trial might still be six months away from the day when Shrien arrived, as he would need to be properly assessed and require time to work with his defence lawyers.

That was fair enough. Shrien probably hadn't been able to sit down with his legal team and plan his defence. I was just relieved that he was going back.

When the day came, Ashok and Anish went to London to deal with the various media requests that had poured in. Representatives from television, radio, newspapers and magazines had all been in touch asking for our reaction as Shrien left.

I didn't want a great deal of fuss and for media people to pour into Mariestad. I wanted to protect our privacy at home and that of our neighbours.

I learned that there was a media circus going on in London, with reporters booking onto Cape Town flights in the hope they would travel with Shrien and, presumably, land exclusive interviews.

But the only exclusivity of the day was the manner in which Shrien eventually travelled. He left Bristol airport at 8pm on April 7 after being taken from the Fromeside Hospital by Metropolitan Police extradition officers and handed over to the South African authorities.

Shrien's mode of transport caused a huge furore and I completely understood why it made the blood of many South Africans boil.

He was given a private charter plane to take him back to face his murder charge. I was amazed at the extent to which the South Africans had gone to pander to his needs.

The bill for his flight was 2,905,574.31 South African rand, which equates to around £161,000 or 1,931,000 Swedish kronor.

The figure was later released by the South African government. In order to give transparency and stave off criticism it said the money had been well spent as Shrien still experienced "suicidal tendencies."

The South Africans felt if Shrien had travelled on a scheduled flight, like the rest of us lesser mortals, it might have compromised his medical condition.

By his side were a doctor, nurse, South African police and Interpol – all essential in getting Shrien to Cape Town without risk, apparently.

I did not agree that spending £161,000 on a private jet to ferry a murder suspect was money well spent. I have never travelled first class so I checked on the web and found first-class private cabins on jets available for £3,000. With all those worries about his health, I suppose I wouldn't have denied him that.

But this chartered plane was a gross waste of money. If I was a South African tax payer I would have been furious. This is a country where there is vast unemployment and many millions live below the poverty line. Crime is rife and medical care for the ordinary man or woman is not always up to international standards, especially in the townships.

Incensed, I did a quick check on the wages of the average citizen and found that the median salary for a debt collector in South Africa was 72,916 rand. What a debt Shrien owed South Africa now. He was surely the first, or one of only a few suspects given such luxury when being brought to face trial.

I couldn't help thinking the move had also been designed to keep the press away from him. If that was true, it was wrong. The media have played a legitimate part in the due process and are given seats in court as witnesses for the public to justice being served. They should have been allowed to witness the end of a three and a half year wait and bring the pictures

233

to the public.

I understood that Shrien's welfare was of prime importance and correctly so. But with police around him it would have only been right to allow the cameramen a few seconds with him.

Nilam and I also wanted to see what he looked like now. It had been a few years since we had set eyes on him and his absence from court had tormented us even further. One reporter said he was expected to fly from Heathrow so the media had assembled there and many had bought tickets for a night flight to Cape Town.

We watched TV news and flicked over repeatedly during the day. Although happy to see Ashok and Anish on the screen, we were disappointed there was no sign of the suspect being taken to South Africa.

My brother and son were extremely smart in delivering measured messages on behalf of the Hindocha family. They stated we were "one step closer" to the truth and only when we had it would Anni be allowed to rest in peace.

Pictures of Anish breaking down in tears reached our television screens in Mariestad. He wept as he said: "I have trouble sleeping, and I know my dad has trouble sleeping. I call him at 3am or 4am and I know he's awake. He can't sleep. It's very difficult for him and I try to be strong for him."

Nilam and I also sobbed as we watched the television. Anish is a very proud and decent young man. He misses Anni terribly. He was six years younger than her and she showered her baby brother with love.

He was only 22 years old when his sister was murdered. Over the years he had grown into a strong man. His strength

for us has been invaluable but he continues to miss her. His
Facebook message for all to see still reads: "There are Angels,
My sister is one of them. I love you Anni Ninna Hindocha.
You are in my heart ♥."

Now here he was, looking smart in a suit, being brave and
honourable, paying tribute to Anni and standing up for us.
My son has a heart that is a carbon copy of Anni's. Generous,
kind, respectful, and loving. Why did he and Ami have to
suffer like this too? Ashok was again the solid backbone, doing
interview after interview and insisting that, at last, the case
should be about Anni and not just Shrien.

We were on the verge of getting the truth and I could not
sleep that night as I waited for news that Shrien was airborne
and on his way to Cape Town.

At breakfast time, I saw Shrien on TV for the first time in
a couple of years. He was wearing a dark suit and looked
greyer than before. Anni used to tell me how much grey
hair he had and that he use to colour it every two weeks.
Now I know what she meant by that. He also looked
skinnier. He had his head down as photographers caught
him disembarking from the jet and being led to the police
car. I cursed under my breath at how much ill luck we had
suffered since he came into our lives.

Waiting for him in Cape town were officers from the elite
Hawks police unit. Among them was Captain Louise Smith,
a tenacious and public-spirited officer who was to prove a
fantastic means of bolstering our confidence when we arrived
in Cape Town.

Shrien's family issued a statement immediately upon his
arrival, saying: "Shrien remains committed to proving his

innocence in a court of law and uncovering the truth behind his wife's murder."

The South African justice department also issued a statement which, although pointing out the obvious, effectively summed up my feelings. It said: "He is not on a honeymoon. He is not on holiday. He is here to stand trial and we want to see that happen within a reasonable period of time."

Shrien duly appeared in court within an hour of touching down in Cape Town. Television and photography had been banned from the building and I was not personally there but I had the vision in my mind that I had waited so long to see.

Shrien Dewani was in the dock at Western Cape High Court, the place he should have been three and a half years ago. The charges were murder, robbery with aggravating circumstances, kidnapping, and defeating the ends of justice.

The victim was Anni Ninna Hindocha, born March 12, 1982, Mariestad, Sweden, died November 13, 2010, Gugulethu. South Africa.

My daughter. My baby. Now we were going to hear the truth about her death.

Chapter 27

The kindness of strangers

Mariestad, Sweden
August, 2014

It went mostly quiet on the Shrien Dewani front for a few months as summer set in and as the Hindocha family began searching for flights and accommodation in Cape Town.

We wanted to concentrate on preparing for Shrien's trial. We had been told to expect a trial of at least two months because of the number of witnesses and legal arguments to be presented. Sneha was confirmed as being one of the key witnesses. Whenever I spoke to her she insisted she was not worried about the prospect of going into the witness box of a major murder trial as part of the case against the man accused of murdering Anni.

She was well aware that she had crucial evidence against Shrien to present to the court and of its importance. Naturally she showed a little nervousness and I realised she was being strong for Anni. It was obviously going to be an ordeal for her. She had largely shied away from interviews, even though her interactions with Anni by email and text had been leaked and made front-page banner headlines.

Sneha met several times with Scotland Yard officers who were working closely with the Cape Town detectives. On a few occasions she went to the South African embassy near Trafalgar Square to brief them for a whole day. They in turn gave her a rundown on how things worked in the court. I was satisfied she would be well looked after and glad that her husband would be accompanying her to Cape Town as support for both her and for us.

The German Master, Leopold Leisser, was also listed to help the prosecution. That was an incredible development. One must remember that for the purposes of confidentiality and protecting evidence, very little information is given to families and we were almost as much in the dark as anybody else.

But Mr Leisser's inclusion brought home a very disturbing message to Nilam and me. The police were going to try to prove in court that Shrien had known this male prostitute. I had read threats of legal action over claims of Shrien being a secret homosexual and the denials. I did not know what to believe and I suppose I locked it away in my mind in order to concentrate on knowing how Anni died. Everything would be revealed in court, which was the right place, as I had consistently maintained.

But this leather-clad gentleman was now to be a key witness and I wondered what he was going to reveal. His presence was, by its very nature, going to be a sensational development. Nick Parker, the reporter who had taped an interview with Shrien at the say-so of Max Clifford, was also mentioned as a prosecution witness. I presumed the police wanted him to reveal to the court what Shrien had – and hadn't – told him.

I understood there were to be police witnesses and

somebody involved with the internet but I had no idea who this person was or how he could help the prosecution.

Also I was aware that my family and I would be under incredible scrutiny from all quarters and the police promised to look after us and shield us from unwanted attention.

It was to be my sixth trip to South Africa since Anni's death. Each of the previous five had proved difficult in their own way. I wondered over and over in my mind how this one would be. The only thing we had confirmed was that Shrien was there and being prepared for trial.

Nilam and I had prepared ourselves for four years with fortnightly psychiatric care. The entire Hindocha family had received wonderful support from people all over the world, particularly Britain and South Africa and, of course, at home in Mariestad.

The letters, emails and posts on social media constantly gave us a lift and I often told Nilam that there were good people in the world, despite the bad people who had taken Anni.

One such good person was a woman from Cape Town who came to see me in Mariestad specifically to offer us her apartment to use. She had been so touched and saddened by Anni's death and had closely followed developments from the first day.

She told me she wanted us to have the most comfortable and secure stay in Cape Town as she realised what a difficult time for us all it was going to be.

She was clearly wealthy and extremely kind. This was demonstrated when she handed me the keys to her apartment there and then. We had only just met. We were strangers. And here she was giving me her home and her support. Of course

I offered to pay her fully, but she was not interested, no matter how much I insisted. I was lost for words.

This amazing stranger, who out of respect for her wishes will remain anonymous, was utterly genuine. I was so touched by this. This was an act of kindness that came out of the blue, from somebody across the world who had been ashamed that people from her home country had killed my daughter.

Nilam and I had already packed a week before we were due to leave. I began when Sky News crime correspondent Martin Brunt came from London to see me with his TV crew and I agreed to be interviewed. I had known about his work on the Madeleine McCann disappearance and had been following his reporting from Portugal and the UK since she went missing in 2007. I watch his channel in Mariestad and I suppose it is the power of television that, when I opened the front door to him, I felt as if I was greeting an old friend.

I was touched that Mr Brunt would travel all the way from the UK to meet me. He was very diplomatic and clearly was genuinely sorry for us and our loss. But despite his sensitivity his questions were nothing new. We had heard the same ones and given the same answers ever since Anni died. We took him to Lake Vänern, where we had scattered our daughter's sacred ashes in the spring of 2011. I also took him to Anni's school and playground. He didn't film the school. I suppose these visits are my way of remembering Anni, showing her old hangouts and talking about her. It does comfort me.

But I did agree when his producer suggested his cameraman might film me opening the suitcase and packing for South Africa.

Nilam and I agreed to take three suitcases between us. I

packed three suits, ten ties and 15 shirts. Three of those shirts were bought for me by Anni. They were my favourites, a blue one, a brown shirt with stripes and a black and white shirt.

The day before we left began with me making a trip to the hospital with Nilam. She was feeling weak and unwell and had a pain in her leg. We went to see doctors at nearby Skövde, a town located 30 km from Mariestad. The visit took seven hours. The doctors were very professional and attentive and gave Nilam prescriptions for medicines that she needed for the trip. We had feared her health was not up to the journey to South Africa and all that was to come during the time we were there.

Luckily the medics passed her fine and fit to travel. I knew she would have gone anyway. But this was never going to be a pleasurable trip. We knew it was going to be very tough.

I got up several times during that final night at home, pacing the bedroom, then into our kitchen and then into the bathroom. I even put the TV on at around 3am and then quickly shut it off. My mind was buzzing and I believe the anticipation had built up in me until it was like a fizzy drink about to explode from its bottle. We were entering a new phase, probably the final one, in our search for the truth.

I still asked myself the question that has preoccupied me since the moment Anni was killed. Why did my daughter have to die? Why was she taken like this?

In the morning I checked the house and turned off all the electrical points. It would be more than two months before Nilam and I were expected to return. I hoped to open my front door when we came back, feeling we could at last begin mourning Anni properly as justice in South Africa had prevailed.

I drove my trusted Mercedes to the home of a friend who lives close to Gothenburg airport. At the airport, people approached us because they recognised us, having seen the news that Shrien's trial was about to begin and that we were on our way. The general sentiment echoed by all the people who approached us was: "Good luck. Good luck," which I appreciated.

Nilam and I boarded a Turkish Airlines flight on Saturday, October 5, at 4.45pm. In less than 48 hours our lives were to change again in the most dramatic way.

I had booked seats 17b and 17d in economy. Although I have worked all my life, am self-made and could have stretched to business class for this trip, I don't believe in wasting money and cannot bring myself to spend it on something when I know I can get through without splashing out vast sums.

I can't explain what it is. I am not tight and will happily spend on others. It might be that I have seen hard times and therefore extravagance is something my family do not indulge in.

As I sat back in my seat, Nilam complained about the pain in her leg. It was swollen. I looked at her and realised again how much she was suffering.

The flight was full and a little cramped. Nilam was given help by the cabin crew in keeping her leg raised. Again, sleep was not really possible. We were exhausted. But it wasn't just physical discomfort.

The flight touched down in Istanbul around 11pm and then was soon airborne again for the 13-and-a-half hour journey to

Cape Town.

I did not know there was a stop-off in Johannesburg but when we were there the high-profile nature of the case began to hit home. Quite a lot of people recognised me. The Shrien saga was on the front pages of the newspapers at the airport. People shook my hands and said: "You'll get justice."

When we landed in Cape Town I felt a surge of trepidation as this was the city where my Anni had been killed so brutally. I looked out of the plane's windows and thought about her landing here on this airstrip and seeing what I was seeing now. I felt tears in my eyes.

I always had a heavy heart each time I landed in Cape Town. It made me go cold, made me lose control of my legs. When I saw signs saying "Welcome to Cape Town" I would always think about Anni and whether her beautiful eyes had chanced upon these things too.

I thought about how four years ago Anni's body had been loaded on to the plane to take her home with me, Shrien and his father Prakash and now here I was again still seeking justice for her.

Cape Town Detective Captain Louise Smith greeted us and she was wearing the same trilby she'd had on her head the first time I met her all those years back. It was always a comforting and familiar sight to meet her.

Captain Smith guided us past the long, winding passport queue and through customs. We felt a little embarrassed to be queue-jumping but I was glad for the small favour as we were very tired. As we walked through immigration, one official whispered: "Good luck, sir."

Outside the terminal we were immediately struck by the

heat and its intensity. It was 27C whereas back home in
Mariestad it was minus 2C. It's funny how such a simple thing
could bring a small smile to my face.

Nilam and I boarded a police minibus which did not have
any markings on the outside. As we took our seats, Captain
Smith told us this was the same vehicle used to transport
Shrien when he had arrived here on his private chartered jet.
Nilam and I were sitting on the same bench that Dewani had
sat on and looked out at the beauty of Cape Town and its
blue skies and sunshine.

To our left was Table Mountain and ahead of us were the
waterfront and the Cape Grace Hotel where Anni spent her
last few days. People were walking through markets and gently
ambling along the streets. Some had stopped to watch an
African dance troupe. In Long Street, people sat outside at
cafe tables chatting. I remember some wonderful music
drifting through our windows as we passed. It appeared to be
a happy place with lovely old buildings overlooked by
mountains.

But Nilam was troubled by the thought of Anni having to
leave this fashionable part of Cape Town where she would
have belonged to visit a run-down place where crime was rife.

Nilam whispered to me: "Why did he take her to a
township? I know my daughter would never say she wanted
to see one."

Cape Town is a beautiful city but I was never going to have
the same pleasure as others at being here. It would never be
a holiday for me, never have the same atmosphere. It would
always be the city where Anni was murdered.

The second-floor flat we had been so generously loaned was

incredibly smart and modern with three bedrooms and a balcony which gave us the most stunning vista. We had a full-on view of Table Mountain with flowers and greenery everywhere we looked. Table Mountain is an amazing sight.

But this was no holiday. Nilam opened the suitcases and settled down to getting used to our home for the next few months. It had a large, wall-mounted television and a nicely equipped kitchen. Every day, a cleaner would call. The apartment was beautifully furnished. There was a pond downstairs and we could hear the soothing noises of the fountain from the balcony.

Nilam and I quickly made friends with the security guards on the front gate, who were briefed to call us before allowing any visitors in as we needed some privacy.

The mornings would begin with me making omelettes for whichever members of the family were staying and we quickly discovered a supermarket nearby on Long Street.

Anish settled into his fitness routine of 50-100 press-ups each morning and Nilam and I would go for a daily walk, taking in the sunshine and chatting to the locals. There was also a pizza restaurant in the locality which we visited for dinner a few times. On other nights we would visit the Canal Walk Shopping Centre for a break. We'd learned over the past four years how important it was to have some sort of normality in our day, even though everything about our existence was anything other than normal.

But right now we were lucky, fortunate that this kind stranger had given us somewhere comfortable and relaxing to stay during the ordeal ahead.

It was also in the perfect place, only a few minutes from the

Western Cape High Court, where the next morning the first of Shrien's real judgment days would begin.

Ashok, who had arrived a few days earlier, accompanied me to the offices of a radio station where he had arranged for us to meet the press. This would be the last time we could talk to the media as we didn't want to interfere with the trial. But we wanted to repay journalists with our help for showing such a prolonged interest in Anni's murder.

In the first few months after Anni's death a friend had advised us that there were two courts, the court of law and the court of public opinion. We could only strive to influence the latter in order to get support for justice. The law would take care of the rest.

We had always tried to be courteous and dignified and above all honest. There were exceptions but the media generally seemed to like us and absolutely understood our grief.

I had still not got used to answering their questions. It took me out of my comfort zone. When I look back now at the various television broadcasts from outside the courts in London and Cape Town I was always sobbing and in tears.

During the flight from Istanbul I had written a prepared statement. Ashok agreed that it would be better if I read that while he answered the questions because I would probably find a press conference very difficult. He was right.

As I read my statement directly from the screen of my mobile phone, my voice gave way and I had to remove my glasses to wipe away tears. Each time I looked up over the many microphones placed in front of me to wipe a tear or catch my breath, I would be greeted with a blaze of light and the popping of a line of flashes. ITN, the BBC, Sky, South Africa's SABC and ENCA all broadcast my words with many other channels also covering the event.

My statement made front pages the next day. I told the assembled 100 or so members of the media: "Thank you all for coming. I am back here in Cape Town where my beautiful daughter Anni was shot dead almost four years ago. My wife Nilam, daughter Ami, son Anish, brother Ashok and Anni's cousin Nishma will also be at the trial tomorrow.

"Since that terrible day it has been a period of torture and we have missed her each and every minute of each and every day. Now that I am back here, all I ask for is the full story and justice.

"I am confident that South Africa will conduct a fair and open trial of Shrien Dewani.

"I am grateful to the many, many thousands of people around the world, particularly from South Africa and Britain, who have supported my family through this time.

"Now it is up to the South African legal system to hear the case and obtain the full story on how my daughter died.

"Please understand that we are unable to make any further comments at all until after the trial has been concluded and I request that you do not approach me or my family while this trial is going on.

"My brother Ashok is here with me to answer your questions now and this will be the last time we speak to you until the end of the trial."

Ashok had a talent for handling the media and developed a rapport with reporters.

He was not to be outdone by a tricky question from a

reporter called Ryan Hooper, who had travelled from London for the Press Association.

He asked Ashok whether Dewani would be welcomed back into the family if he was cleared. Ashok snapped back: "No comment."

It was the type of question in which we would be damned if we did and damned if we didn't. Ashok's response was fitting. He also repeated that Anni had become the "daughter of the world" and we had come to Cape Town seeking only the truth and justice.

Ashok had developed a bond of trust with the ENCA TV's Cape Town-based television reporter Leigh-Anne Jansen, who had followed the story of Anni's murder since it happened.

He invited her to our apartment to interview Nilam and me as a thank-you for the way she had reported on the case and kept us informed over the four years.

But we forgot to tell Captain Smith. As she drove us back to the flat her Hawk special unit training kicked in and she suddenly swerved into a side road and did a U-turn to shake off a car which she noticed had been following us. Ashok told her it was Leigh-Anne and her camera team. The dramatic situation actually made us laugh and it lifted the tension a little.

The interview was perfectly straightforward and that night we saw her exclusive interview being broadcast on the giant TV screen. It was curious seeing yourself on television in the very flat where you were interviewed.

We pulled the curtains together and went to bed. Nights were difficult. We didn't sleep much. Anish and Ami had just arrived and were also collected from the airport by Captain

Smith. It was great to see them. We were all here, Nilam, Ami, Anish and Ashok. There was much to talk about still but we had to try to force ourselves to sleep because of the colossal day ahead.

We slept a little, got up, slept some more, got up... and soon daylight was coming through.

By now we were hours away from seeing Shrien again. It had been two years since I last set eyes on him in person. It was going to be a hard moment for us all.

Captain Smith picked us up and took us to meet the Cape Town prosecutors Rodney de Kock and Adrian Mopp in their offices at 8.30am, 90 minutes before we were to at last see Dewani in the dock.

The two gentlemen updated us about how they were going to present the case and seemed very prepared. Rodney told me that for four months his team had been working day and night on the case against Shrien.

Adrian Mopp told us: "We are well prepared and we will do our best."

I felt confident that they had done their research. They also warned us they were going to show a video of when Anni's body was found and that it would be very, very painful.

The lawyers told us they felt they had a pretty good case and a good chance of convicting Dewani of Anni's murder.

I felt sick with nerves. Nilam was no better. My legs turned to jelly and I felt them giving way as we walked out of their offices and to the car to take us to court.

When we pulled up outside Western Cape Court at around 9.50am it was mayhem.

There were dozens and dozens of TV crews, photographers

and reporters. It felt very uncomfortable in a way, all these people taking pictures. But fortunately they acceded to our wishes and didn't ask us any questions.

Now we were here. It had taken four years. The time had come. I prayed for justice to be given to us at last.

Chapter 28

Shrien is in the dock

Cape Town, South Africa
October, 2014

Shrien walked into the court wearing a dark suit and black tie. His hair was now distinctly greyer and he emerged from the staircase below and into the dock looking purposeful and in full possession of his wits.

I felt a sudden rage at the sight of this man. My Anni was left in her hour of need by her so-called husband. How could he have left her like that? Most men would have stayed with their wives, protected them and sacrificed themselves for her freedom. Most men would have remained in that vehicle at all costs instead of surrendering to those hitmen. Most men would have shielded their women with their own bodies from any bullet.

But this was Mr Shrien Dewani, a self-absorbed individual. His own safety had been far more important than Anni's life. How could he have left her like that and stand here now in front of me, head held up high and looking imperturbable?

Shrien's briefcase and documents were carried by others to the dock. He didn't look like a man who had been lost to the world for four years in a state of mental breakdown. He didn't look like he was grieving over the loss of Anni as I was.

If it wasn't for the distance of 6ft between us and the fact that he was surrounded by police and court officials I might well have got to my feet, climbed up into the dock, raised my hand behind my ear and brought it down onto his cheek with a good slap.

Nilam, who sat beside me with her painful leg stretched out on a chair provided for her comfort, looked into my eyes. I could see it was a sign from her that I needed to be calm. I almost had to sit on my hands as the judge began the final chapter in our quest for justice.

Shrien's family were seated on the right side of the dock and on the opposite part of the court, almost as if both families had been strategically placed as far apart as possible and out of each other's direct line of sight.

Prakash was there next to Shila. Preyen took a seat behind Shrien's defence team, alongside the dock, and handed over handwritten notes to them.

There were three media sections, one to our left, one diagonally opposite us and a third behind the dock. They were crammed, each journalist having a media accreditation hanging from their neck. I was told there had been hundreds of media applications and only a tenth had been granted.

The public gallery was above the court and looked directly down on to the judge, Jeanette Traverso, and her two advisers. It too was completely full.

The lawyers were between the judge and Shrien. Security and police added to the claustrophobic feel of the windowless court room in which there was little natural light.

Mr de Kock had surprised me after I landed in Cape

Town when he disclosed that he would not be leading the prosecution or appearing in court as part of the team at all. I was stunned because he had been to several of the extradition hearings in London and had been my main point of contact throughout. It was never made clear to me why Mr Mopp was going to be the lead prosecutor and not Mr de Kock. I assumed that as Director of Public Prosecutions Mr de Kock had other fish to fry.

As Mr Mopp outlined the offences, Shrien stared down at the charge sheet over the prosecutor's shoulder and followed the words as they were relayed to the court, his eyes moving from line to line along the charge sheet. Mr Mopp addressed Shrien as sir.

The charges were conspiracy to kidnap Anni, in contravention of the 1956 Riotous Assemblies Act, with Tongo, Qwabe and Mngeni. Then followed the accusations of kidnap itself, robbery, obstructing the administration of justice and towards the end, almost as an aside, the charge of murdering Anni. He denied all charges and responded: "I plead not guilty to all five counts, my lady."

That was entirely expected and I settled back to hear the prosecution give us the definitive story of how Anni died, Shrien's involvement and how he was going to defend himself.

But instead of the prosecution putting its case first, it was Shrien who surprised us by addressing the court straight away.

His lawyer, Mr Francois van Zyl, read a witness statement and it came across as if Shrien wanted to get something off his chest immediately.

Apparently, Shrien wanted to provide the court with "a synopsis to explain why" he was pleading not guilty to the charges.

What was to come next was a bombshell and it left the six members of the Hindocha family who heard it reeling.

Mr Van Zyl read from Shrien's statement and this is what he said: "I have had sexual interaction with both males and females. I consider myself to be bisexual. My sexual relations with males were mostly physical experiences or email chats with people I met online or in clubs including prostitutes such as Leopold Leisser."

In a few short sentences, Shrien had succeeded in confirming that he had a hunger for gay sex and paid male prostitutes. By his own admission he had also told us he was a liar, a deceitful and secretive individual who had no respect for my daughter's morals and little morality of his own.

This was the first time I had actual confirmation that my son-in-law was not at all the person that he had led us to believe when he courted and married Anni.

Yes, we had read reports about him being gay, but this was coming from his own mouth via his lawyer in the court room.

It is difficult to discuss this point without the risk of sounding like a homophobe and I state again, I am not at all against gay people.

But to hear that the man who married your daughter had a secret sex life with other men is nothing short of horrifying. I shudder when I think about the type of activities he paid for with The German Master. If he was so into this stuff, was this why he and Anni so rarely shared a bed?

Nilam was shaking. Anish, Ami and cousin Nishma were snarling as Mr van Zyl skipped past the devastating points he had just made in a matter-of-fact fashion.

I couldn't make out what else he said for a few minutes while the details of the appalling and fraudulent characteristics of the man seated in the dock finally sank in.

I was angry beyond words. But all I could do was sit and try to look as impassive as possible as I knew all eyes would be on me. I saw some members of the media shaking their heads in disbelief as others wrote reports on their laptops and mobiles, some updating the world through Twitter.

Most people in that courtroom would probably have felt some sympathy for me because of this utter deception. But I was more heartbroken for Anni. She was as innocent as they come and she had been taken in by this Shrien creature.

Her softness and sweet, unsuspecting nature would have been a pushover for Shrien. I now knew why he had caused her all those problems by rejecting her and refusing to sleep with her.

He was into men and Anni would have had absolutely no knowledge or suspicion of this. She would not have tolerated it and she would not have married him if she had known about his true sexuality.

Anni was a modern, but at the same time a cultural, woman who I am sure had gay friends she respected and did not judge at all. But she wanted children and would have believed she was marrying a straight man.

Shrien's secret would have been the last thing she suspected of him even when he pushed her away repeatedly. He had concealed his private life and taken in Anni and all of the Hindocha family.

People marry and can turn out to be lazy, job-shy, alcoholics,

adulterers or even violent abusers. Shrien was none of these.
He was something else which no father could have prepared
for in his list of common anxieties when agreeing to give his
daughter's hand in marriage.

But all the problems in their relationship, the arguments,
the break-ups and the acrimony, fitted now. The puzzle was
beginning to fall into place in the most distasteful manner.

I wondered how we had missed this. What a bolt from the
blue. My poor Anni had been pulled into Shrien's bleak and
desperate life.

Shrien went on, in his "plea explanation" to tell of how he
had met Anni and "was instantly physically attracted to her,
loved her bubbly personality and sensed that there was a
mutual chemistry."

I was amazed at how within a few seconds of delivering his
revelations of liaisons with male prostitutes, online encounters
and gay club meetings, he could move immediately back to his
story of love for Anni.

Shrien went further and his lawyer told the court of his
client's abnormally low hormone levels which had given
him reproduction problems. He underwent testosterone
replacement therapy, which he had been warned had a
number of side-effects such as "blood clots, sleep apnea, mood
swings, breast enlargement, hair loss, acne and weight gain."

He decided to go ahead with the treatment because "having
my own family was important to me."

Really, I asked myself as I listened to his clever summary of
why he was innocent. And this was all before any evidence of
prosecution had been put to the judge. I wondered if all this
might have been too clever. It was a pre-emptive strike. But it

was highly unusual and the judge would surely make a note of that.

He even produced a personal email he had written to Anni after they had rowed on May 24, 2010. Now he was using private correspondence between them to head off the prosecution charges.

His email to Anni, given to the court, read:

Dear Anni,

I think it is better if I write this rather than say it on the phone as then you can read it over and over. I am really upset after our conversation.

I realise we are very different but I have always believed in a relationship you can work through those differences.

When we first met I immediately liked you... And no not just because you are pretty... but because you made me laugh. We had such a good time at the first dinner at Asia de Cuba.

I have always wanted a girl I can be friends with. One that understands me – and I know that is not easy. I know that I am so focused that some people think I am intense. I am focused on achieving things in life. I want to be someone who can do things – and that is not just about making money, but it is about having a rounded social life. A family, a business, an input into the community. When we first met and started dating I knew that you were that girl.

It does need to be right for both of us though. I can't believe that I'm gonna write this, and I actually have tears in my eyes as I write it, but if you really think being with me is not going to make you happy then this is not right for you.

I really hope that is not what you are saying but I don't want to feel like I have forced you into something.

I really do love you, and hence I don't want you to be unhappy. I want to be with you forever but not if that makes you unhappy.

I am really sorry that I have made you feel like this. You are so precious to me – I know I don't always show it. I often find it difficult to show how much you mean to me but please do not think this is because I don't love you.

Speak to you later.

Love always.

Shrien

My stomach turned at the words he used to tell the court of his love for Anni. If he truly loved her, surely he would have stayed with her when the killers ordered him out of the taxi and certainly not deceived her about his sexuality.

Shrien told of the disagreements that preceded the wedding and how Anni wanted to call it off after a row on September 21 during which she said he was controlling. But he had got in touch with me to "calm her down."

As I sat listening to this I wished I hadn't got involved on his behalf and thought if only Anni could have had her way.

There was no mention of the tension at the wedding, merely the fact that it had taken place.

He then recalled how he had taken Anni to the Chitwa Chitwa Game Lodge in Kruger National Park and then on to Cape Town for the second part of the honeymoon where he employed Tongo at the airport.

Much of what Shrien went on to say was about changing money, talking to Tongo about a helicopter ride with Anni and about where to go for dinner. He even mentioned the international chef Jamie Oliver, who had visited a restaurant near Gugulethu. Tongo took them both to see it.

I was expecting Shrien to give us the details of what

happened to Anni before he left her alone with the killers after he and Tongo were no longer in the vehicle.

If this was the explanation of his not guilty plea, then surely now would be the time to tell us what happened. But no, he was having none of it.

When, I wondered, would he tell us what happened? He had taken the bold decision to reveal all this before the prosecution opened, to tell his side. But it was only a partial story.

He went on to say: "As a consequence of the traumatic experience which resulted in the loss of my wife I have been hospitalised for over three years and suffered from severe post-traumatic stress disorder. This, and the resultant flashbacks, nightmares and anxiety attacks, have affected my memory and impacted on my ability to precisely and chronologically recall events concerning this terrible incident."

There you had it. He was going to tell us only what he wanted and because of his illnesses his memory had been impaired.

He described how they had been for dinner and while travelling back their taxi was hijacked.

He went on: "We were both terrified and immediately complied with demands. I was lying half on top of Anni. Another person was behind the steering wheel."

Shrien said one of the attackers turned his attention to him.

"He placed the gun against my left ear and said words to the effect that I should not lie to him or he would shoot me.

"I heard a clicking noise from the gun which scared me even more. I have never been close to a real gun before."

Nor had Anni ever been in such close proximity to a gun.

When Shrien said the attackers were going to let them go separately I saw another extension of his cowardice.

If the attackers were going to let them go separately, then why did he not make sure his wife was freed first? Women and children first, Mr Dewani.

Anni was a woman screaming for her life and that should have resonated with her husband. He should have thought about her safety first and foremost. In a similar situation I know for a fact that I would never leave Nilam alone. Nobody lays a finger on my wife and I suppose that phrase "Over my dead body" is appropriate here.

What happened next is well known. Shrien and Tongo survived. Anni was shot dead.

I was glad when the judge adjourned for a 15 minute tea break, which was to become the norm each day.

Nilam and I left for a side room and we could hardly speak to each other, such was the shock and sense of betrayal we shared.

It was clear now that the prosecution were going to use details of Shrien's secret sex life to prove the motive for murdering Anni.

He was, on the surface, a "good Hindu boy", but now he was going to have to face up to the claim that he married her to disguise his sordid background and had used her.

I wondered whether Anni had discovered his hidden true self during their honeymoon in South Africa and was about to expose him. Could this be why she met her death?

Back in the court I stared long and hard at Shrien as he re-entered. He would not look at me. I was full of contempt for him. Horrified. Sickened. Angry.

Overwhelmingly I was disgusted at the deception of Anni much more than anything else.

Chapter 29

There are things a parent should never have to see

Cape Town, South Africa
October, 2014

Sadly I am unable to present an accurate record of what happened in court next. I had faced everything in the four years since Anni was taken from us. Absolutely every difficult piece of information, attended nearly every hearing and been there when the law dealt with the three killers.

It was my duty as Anni's father and the head of my family to be strong and carry the biggest burden of grief.

But on the first day of Shrien's trial, every single member of the Hindocha family understood why I had to walk out of the hearing.

There are some things that a parent maybe should not have to see. Nilam and I had been advised that a video to be shown after the lunch break would be of the crime scene – exactly as it was left by the killers.

Anni's body, lying slain by a gunshot, would be shown in graphic and absolute detail.

We decided to stay outside the court as the film was shown because it would, understandably, be too distressing for us. The officials had begun installing a television and re-arranging

the court during the break and we knew what was coming
next.

I hoped this phase of the trial would pass quickly and
without any further embarrassing technical hitches.

I had already been maddened at the poor quality of the
sound from the microphones and the court speaker system
and the judge had declared that she felt the same. The court
had to take two breaks while the equipment was tested and
attempts made to improve the sound.

I was so infuriated that I rose to my feet at the second
interruption and offered to examine and rectify the problem
myself using my experience as an electrical engineer.

Sighs of disappointment came from around the court as the
judge berated officials, including Mr Mopp. And yet another
adjournment had taken place.

The judge left the court for a short break, ordering staff to
sort out the mess. After she had disappeared through à door to
her left, chaos ensued.

It was an embarrassing moment for the prosecution, after
all, a very serious murder trial and an examination of my
daughter's death was on hold due to microphone problems.

We sat there as a family bewildered at the insensitivity of
it all. It just deepened our anxiety and we became more
annoyed when one security official entered the witness box
and began testing the microphone by repeating numbers. The
public gallery was also irritated as it was in everyones interest
to get this trial going.

The South Africans had been given four years to prepare for
this trial. The world was watching and they knew that. And
they still couldn't organise a simple microphone and speaker

to enable the important evidence to be relayed properly to all.

Ashok and I discussed how these type of issues hardly filled us with confidence and did not bode well for everything else that was to come from the state.

I hoped there would be no similar cock-ups when it came to showing the film of Anni's murder scene which was certain to be harrowing for my family.

Indeed it was. Ashok, Anish, Nishma and Ami decided they had to see it, with Ami declaring that she had to know every detail about Anni's death and witness every piece of evidence herself before she could begin to come to terms with it.

The court fell respectfully silent as the screens showed Tongo's silver VW Sharan parked on a street in the sunshine. My family later informed me that the first sign of there being something wrong, dreadfully wrong in fact, was when the camera zoomed on to a patch of Anni's dried blood on the sill of the car, underneath the passenger door.

Ami and Anish gasped and cried as the cameraman then opened the door, to reveal Anni's lifeless body lying side on, with her face down into the seat. She was dressed for a night out in her black French Connection evening dress and high heels. Not for some less fancy meal and visit to a township far from the Cape Grace Hotel.

My daughter's hair billowed in the wind as the door was opened and the camera panned around her, almost as if it giving her life. But she had been left for dead. Killed by two hitmen and left by her husband.

I am told that during the hour Nilam and I were absent there was not a sound to be heard in the courtroom apart from that of my family's grief. I appreciated that respect.

Those that saw the video said the fact that the cameraman's hand was shaking as he filmed gave the scene a harsher reality. The only sound was the rush of wind and the opening of the car door.

I was relieved that Nilam and I were not there to witness those images and that we will never have to see them. That is not how we want to remember Anni.

Ashok told me that a member of the media mentioned to him afterwards that he had been to places on assignments where he had to count bodies, but seeing the film of Anni, a beautiful, young and innocent woman lying there like that would haunt him forever.

I was glad that we took the decision not to view the film. There is a bit of me that thinks perhaps I should have seen it but I am confident that it is part of the picture of Anni's death that others can paint for me. It is just too painful to think about, let alone see for myself. I had seen Anni's body on the day after her murder and that was devastating enough. I just felt it was unnecessary for me, and particularly for Nilam, to put ourselves through it. I was sure it would be too much for Anni's mother, even though I had pictured the scene in my mind a thousand times or more.

After we had taken our seats again, I did find some comfort from the words of Dr Janet Vester, the pathologist, who said the shot delivered to Anni's neck meant she would have been dead "in a few heartbeats" because of massive blood loss.

I was thankful that my daughter would have known very little pain and suffered for only a few seconds before dying. The gunshot would have been like turning off a light with a flick of a switch. Please God, let there have been no pain for her.

Dr Vester's expert opinion was that the 9mm gun that killed her was held between 10 and 25 centimetres from her neck. Anni was shot like an animal, but it was over in a few seconds and she was left dying in agony alone in that taxi.

The pathologist also gave us the news that Anni's spinal cord had been shattered to such an extent that it would have rendered her paralysed if she had lived.

Dr Vester then allayed my worst fears when she confirmed there were no signs of sexual assault or rape of Anni. There had been some disgraceful reporting that she may have been sexually assaulted. At least this had now been dismissed definitively.

Still, these were distressing details to have to listen to. We had prepared ourselves. We knew that this was going to be a long trial with so many details to be covered.

Also it was probably helpful that we couldn't make out every word that was said as the extent of Anni's injuries were revealed. The defence were keen to question the pathologist about finger marks on Anni's leg and she said my daughter may have resisted the attackers. I wondered how Shrien's counsel was going to use this information later.

I glared long and hard at Qwabe when he entered the room to give evidence, sandwiched between two guards, his arms resting on the shoulders of the first as a security measure.

He began by admitting he had been part of the gang that killed Anni and was serving a 25-year sentence handed down to him in August 2012.

I hated him from the moment I first heard about him all those years ago, and I hated him more today as I looked at this puny and evil individual across the court room. Although he looked like a little child he had killed my daughter.

That he was helping the prosecution was a good thing, I thought. But he was in it only for himself, as we later discovered when Mr van Zyl informed the court why we had been delayed at the start of the day. Apparently, Qwabe had refused to take the witness stand at the last minute unless the prosecutors promised to lop a few more years from his sentence.

I just hoped he would tell the truth about how he came to be one of four men in the vehicle that night with Anni.

Qwabe said he and Mngeni had been put in touch with Tongo by Monde Mbolombo, who told him: "There was a husband who wanted his wife to be killed."

The next day Tongo met with Qwabe and Mngeni and a price of 15,000 rand had been agreed, which at that time was around £1,300. That was all these men needed to take Anni's life.

He said they had to make it look like a hijacking and that Tongo and Shrien were to be released unharmed.

How Anni's taxi came to be stopped at that junction in Gugulethu was already well documented. But I was learning new facts each time he spoke. He wore a pair of yellow kitchen gloves when he kidnapped Anni.

He revealed that after they had taken Anni a police car passed them. I whispered to Nilam how unfortunate it was that the police didn't chance upon them and stop the car. After Tongo and Shrien had been released, Mngeni shot Anni. Qwabe told us: "I heard a gunshot. After the gunshot I got a shock. Mngeni said, 'I shot the lady.' I pulled over on to the pavement and stopped the car. I saw she was on the back seat of the car."

He didn't even check if she was dead or alive and went to look for the bullet casing before throwing it into a storm drain. The money for Anni's murder was in a pouch in the car. There was 10,000 rand and he said they relieved Shrien of a further 4,000 rand.

Given the vile nature of this individual, I was not surprised to hear him say that he went out with friends after shooting Anni "because it was a Saturday evening."

So a murder was almost routine for him, despite the devastation that single act went on to cause. I felt concerned, however, when Mr van Zyl elicited from him that he had lied under oath at a bail hearing before he confessed to being involved in Anni's death.

If Shrien was indeed guilty and was to be ultimately convicted, then the judge would have to be persuaded that witnesses like Qwabe would be credible as witnesses. He and Tongo had pointed the finger at Shrien. To prove his involvement, the court would have to believe the word of convicted killers.

The prosecution had been confident from the start and certain of Shrien's involvement. However with men like Tongo and Qwabe they were going to have their work cut out to convince the court.

I knew these men were unlikely to be impressive witnesses, and that their evidence would be attacked by Shrien's defence, mainly on the fact that they were proven to be ruthless killers, convicted of taking a young woman's life for a pocketful of rand.

But I had come to hear the truth. As Anni's father, I demanded it. Qwabe being revealed as a liar and confessing that he had earlier lied under oath was not a good omen. I wondered what else the prosecution had up its sleeve.

Chapter 30

"Please allow us the full story"

Cape Town, South Africa
October, 2014

Shrien Dewani is gay. He says so himself in his profile, written by him, for a dating website for homosexual men. This was revealed by Simon Johnson, a digital product manager who used to work for the website Gaydar, where men interested in other men can chat online and meet each other for fulfilment.

I had never heard of it before but was informed that it is a meeting point where one pays to be in touch with men who have similar needs. Shrien had listed himself as a single gay man and paid £60 in March 2010 to maintain his membership – eight months before Anni was murdered.

He had been with Gaydar for six years, having first joined in August 2004. I could feel my blood boiling as the details of his dishonesty to Anni were revealed.

Shrien had met Anni in May 2009 and, despite the break-ups and rows, was seeing Anni and deceiving her at the same time as he continued to be a member of Gaydar.

I had been slightly confused from the moment on the first morning when Shrien told the court in his plea explanation:

"I consider myself to be bisexual."

The confirmation of his sexuality or conflict within himself had come as a complete and unwelcome surprise to me. There were to be further shocks.

In the witness box Mr Johnson, who had been flown to Cape Town by the prosecution, revealed Shrien had used the moniker "Asiansubguy" when signing on to the site and engaging with others. This term had to be spelled out to the judge.

The terms Asian and guy were not new. But the use of the word "sub" was later revealed to me to be referring to somebody who was "submissive" in their sexual preferences. Nilam and I were still puzzled as to what it could mean. He also listed himself as "passive."

So I was outraged when it was revealed that Shrien had been surfing Gaydar twice on November 12, 2010, as he and my daughter waited for their flight from Johannesburg to Cape Town.

I took that as a gross insult to Anni, who should have been able to expect the undivided attention of her husband on their honeymoon. He couldn't have had much interest in her if was surfing the gay dating website during what should have been a special time for them both.

What a terrible thing to do to your loving wife of only two weeks. Shame on him.

I could not see Shrien's face because of our positions in court but I saw a tweet from the media later which said he had stifled a yawn at the very moment these details were being given. Clearly, he had no shame.

Then Anish had to hold me back from rising to my feet

when we learned that his computer had been logged on to the site for three separate hours on November 15, two days after Anni had been killed.

Shrien had surfed Gaydar while I waited at the Cape Grace Hotel to collect Anni's body. That it so heartless and disrespectful. I did recall him being on his laptop when he sat opposite me in the hotel lounge and I shuddered at his utter disregard for Anni and my family. How could he have done that? His wife had been shot dead after he left her. Yet while his father-in-law was sitting with him, completely lost in grief, all he could think of was sex? I had no sympathy for Shrien at all by now, just contempt.

Apparently he had also signed into a fetish website called Recon at about the same time. I checked what Recon was later and read the website's introduction: "Recon is mastering the fetish evolution with millions of gay men worldwide into fetish sex. Connect and discover new kinks with other men."

What it added up to was that this brazen individual had insulted Anni and shown little respect for her or me. Further mockery of Anni's good name was disclosed the next morning by Mark Roberts of the UK Police National Cyber Crime Unit, who examined Shrien's Dell laptop and found 53 emails between him and a man whose name was not revealed. Some were of a graphic sexual nature but others referred to his upcoming marriage to Anni.

One email from the unnamed man told Shrien: "Marriage is a serious commitment, not just because of the marriage but because it usually involves children."

Mr Roberts also said he had gone into the laptop to examine Shrien's activity by using key search words such as names of places in South Africa and "gay, fetish, rubber and watersports."

There was an astonishing intervention by the judge, who stopped Mr Roberts's evidence and stated that Mr Dewani's sexuality and the emails were "irrelevant" to the murder charge.

Mr Mopp rose to his feet to say Shrien "was conflicted about whether to get married or come out" and that is why the witness should be allowed to continue. I could see this was going to be a major turning point in the trial when the judge questioned whether his indecision over marriage was "a motive to kill."

Shrien's defence counsel insisted the emails should only be referenced in connection with his "cold feet" over getting married and were otherwise not relevant. The judge came down firmly on Shrien's side when she told the court: "Whether he is bisexual or gay does not matter. It is irrelevant."

Mr Mopp tried sticking to his guns by stating: "The sexuality of the accused is not something we can run away from in this matter. There is a particular factual matrix in this case."

I could feel the tension in the court rising as she hit back: "And what does that provide… motive to kill? You have got to be careful, Mr Mopp. You can't sneak in through the back door what you can't get in through the front."

And that was that. The prosecution's chief evidence regarding motive had been rejected and we were only in the first few days of the trial.

I would have liked to have heard more about Shrien's sexual deviancy in order to confirm what a defective husband he was likely to have been to my Anni had she lived.

I could see the case against Shrien further falling apart when Judge Traverso banned The German Master prostitute Leopold Leisser from telling the court about his three sadomasochistic sessions with Shrien.

He had been called to testify about Shrien discussing his forthcoming wedding to Anni and how he needed to "find a way out."

But the court sent Leisser packing, ruling much of his evidence as 'irrelevant' because Shrien had already revealed his secret sexuality. I disagreed strongly with the rejection of this evidence. I believed it was the court's duty to hear all witnesses fully and then make a ruling what to accept and reject after the defence and prosecution had their say.

It was later reported that Shrien had paid Leisser to racially abuse him and invited him to carry out the most abusive type of activity involving urine and nipple clips, which made him bleed. This was revealed in Leisser's statement listed in court documents.

But the prosecution's battle to present a convincing case was to be severely tested again as there were clearly unsatisfactory contradictions in evidence given by South African police witnesses.

Warrant Officer Peter Engelbrecht, a police ballistics expert, was derided by the defence. While re-constructing the layout of Tongo's vehicle he used a different kind of car. And there were more mistakes in a film he made.

It felt as though the prosecution case was going down the pan. They still had Sneha and Tongo to come, of course, but as we sat eating our meal in an Italian restaurant that evening we agreed that the case was swinging firmly Shrien's way.

The journalist Nick Parker also came to the court and was in the witness box for an hour. He said Shrien had threatened to sue his newspaper, The Sun, if it connected him with The German Master, the male prostitute who was based in Birmingham. But Parker's interview appeared and Shrien never took any legal action against him.

While all this was going on Mngeni had died from brain cancer in a Cape Town prison hospital. I was angered that South African television covered his funeral as if he was some kind of statesman. He was a cruel killer and I would have preferred that he was given the funeral he deserved and buried without any fuss. He had escaped a life sentence and had pleaded with the court to be released a few months earlier on compassionate grounds. I had been asked by the South African authorities for my views on whether I would approve of him being freed. I strongly disagreed since this was the man who shot my daughter and it would not be just to let him out of prison regardless of his medical condition. My reason was that even doctors can be wrong. How can you be sure that a person would die after a certain period of time? He could have lived for several years as far as I was concerned. He took a life - why should he be given his freedom?

Nilam and I were extremely proud of Sneha when she took the witness box next. We knew she was nervous. This brave young woman had been made to wait four years before being allowed to tell the court of the poor way Shrien had treated her best friend and cousin.

She had missed Anni as much as we had. They were inseparable and I know Sneha longed for Anni to be there when she had her own wedding. I hoped that this opportunity to tell the world about Shrien's treatment of Anni would also be liberating for her.

Her husband, who had met Anni once in the early days of his relationship with Sneha, was sitting with us as his wife entered the witness box and I could see his presence was a confidence boost for her.

Sneha said Shrien and Anni fought a lot and confirmed that Anni had been surprised when Shrien's family greeted Nilam and me with the silver thali as a blessing and engagement announcement when we went to their home for the first and only time.

Anni had wanted to call off the engagement but Shrien won her over as always after promising to change his ways.

All the problems between the couple, sexual and emotional, were spilled out during two days of her testimony. I had to wipe tears from my eyes as Sneha relayed how Anni wanted a divorce and told her she did not want to travel to South Africa.

Sneha had advised her to go on the honeymoon and "try and resolve" the issues. If this failed, Sneha said, she would put some money into Anni's Swedish account for an air ticket home. All Anni had to do was dial Sneha's mobile, hang up and the money would be deposited.

But Anni was going to live with the family so she thought that after the stress from the wedding and after having spent time with all of the Dewani's once back from India, it may be good for them to have some time alone. If Sneha would have advised her not to go then I am still sure that Shrien would have persuaded her one way or the other.

But Anni had sent four text messages, the last one saying that "things were going better" and Sneha said she had felt relieved.

Sneha recalled the awful behaviour of Shrien at Anni's funeral and that she believed he was "lying about the sequence of events surrounding Anni's murder."

She knew Anni well enough to know that she would have no interest in going to visit a township after dark dressed as she was in that black party dress...

She also told how she was disturbed by Shrien's lack of grieving and sadness over Anni's death. He was simply not behaving like that of a grieving husband. Her suspicions were raised so much that she secretly recorded him talking about Anni's death.

The defence had tried to portray the couple as happy and planning a baby, even producing medical evidence from a doctor. I had been angered at this claim as well as the revelation that Anni's private medical records had been obtained.

I was Anni's next of kin so how could Shrien have been given her medical records? Sneha was adamant that no such pregnancy had been planned.

I turned to Anish and said: "How could he plan to make her pregnant when he was busy with his gay sex life and not sleeping with her?"

Sneha went on to say that Anni had told her Shrien had problems getting an erection and that she had tried to initiate sex with him but failed.

This was an important part of the case as it showed the extent of the problems there had been.

My guilt at not stopping the union deepened during the trial. As she spoke I put my head in my hands and prayed to Anni in heaven to forgive me again for not seeing the warning signs. In my worst nightmares I just could not have envisaged an ending like this for her.

Divorce would have been perfectly acceptable to me if Anni had come to me and said she had made a mistake. I would still have had my Anni. If only.

When Zola Tongo took the witness stand, I felt that it would interesting to hear his testimony for the first time. This man had ruined his life and his family's future by getting involved in this murder plot. Now he had an 18-year sentence to serve and all for a few measly rand.

He was the only one of the three convicted men to have actually spoken with Shrien. He claimed he had quite simply been approached at Cape Town airport to organise the hit by Shrien. He had stated to Tongo that he wanted somebody "taken out of sight."

But his story of how he had engaged Qwabe and Mngeni, had meetings with them and then arranged the murder through Mbolombo was torn apart by Shrien's defence.

His counsel managed to convince the judge that Tongo was a poor witness who had changed his story from statements made at previous hearings when the three convicted killers had been tried.

The fact that Shrien had handed him cash in a plastic bag at the Cape Grace, which had been caught on CCTV, was said by the defence to show Shrien's caring side.

He had only been enquiring about Tongo's wellbeing and had paid for the taxi driver's legitimate services because he felt

sorry for him. He had also bought him a thank-you card. It
all sounded ridiculous to me, that a man who has lost his wife
in such terrible circumstances would buy a thank-you card for
his taxi driver when most would expect him to be in a state of
shock.

I felt Tongo's evidence may have been plausible to some
because of its simplicity and that he had no reason to want
to help convict an innocent man, but the inaccuracies were
numerous and easily exposed by Mr van Zyl.

All three killers had given different or incomplete versions of
what happened. I knew all three were imprisoned murderers
and that in the eyes of the law Shrien was an innocent man
until convicted. I had come prepared to listen to the evidence
with an open mind. But his defence heavily implied that the
three were ruthless killers and that Shrien was being framed
and was of good character.

As Tongo was torn apart in the witness box I could see by
the look on the judge's face that she found him extremely
unconvincing. After his evidence was complete, my family and
I hardly spoke. We were stunned at the ease with which the
prosecution was being swept aside.

They had put forward a motive in that Shrien was
struggling with his sexuality and preferred men. They showed
he had surfed gay sex websites while with Anni, and hours
after her death. They showed him paying cash secretly to the
taxi driver, and they claimed Shrien and Tongo exchanged
text messages on the night of the murder in the build-up to
her death.

But they failed in the old-fashioned sense of producing
something akin to a finger print from Shrien which would

have placed him in the centre of that gang without any doubt.

Mbolombo, who had been given immunity from prosecution, also admitted he lied about the extent of his role in his evidence during Mngeni's trial.

Previously he claimed only to have introduced the gang members to each other acting as a middleman in the plot. But here he confirmed he co-ordinated the attack, in a series of phone calls on the night of the carjacking, after the first attempt of the gunmen to meet the taxi had failed.

The judge was unimpressed and warned Mbolombo that she would be re-examining his right to immunity.

The fourth anniversary of Anni's death arrived and court was adjourned for the day to allow us to mourn. Once again we visited the spot where her body was found. I had been there several times. This time Anish also joined me and we prayed and laid roses in her memory.

The car was found on the roadside but Nilam and I had previously laid flowers on a barren piece of land a few feet away from the spot. It seemed more appropriate.

Now a house stood there and we were kindly given permission by the house owner to put flowers on her land.

Nilam and I led the prayers with a Hindu priest and there were dozens of media in waiting when we arrived. Thankfully, all were respectful. We had made an earlier visit here with Ami, Ashok, Nishma and Sneha and that proved a tearful occasion too. But it was necessary. I suppose it is a way of us feeling closer to Anni as the manner in which she died robbed us of the chance to say goodbye.

Back in court the defence applied, under section 174 of South Africa's Criminal Procedures Act, to have the charges against Shrien dismissed.

What they were saying was Shrien had absolutely no case to answer and he should be allowed to go back home a free man.

I could not believe this was about to happen. All I had ever asked for was the full story of how Anni died. There had been inconsistencies in Shrien's story which, at the very least, needed clearing up.

They couldn't let him walk away without giving us the whole truth. This was only half a case and I could not believe what was being asked. I felt as if I was about to suffer another injustice after losing Anni. I wanted Shrien to stand there in front of the court and tell us what happened, once and for all. I wanted him to be examined by the state prosecution, since there were so many questions he needed to answer to.

The judge adjourned the case for a fortnight to examine the application and made it clear that she was not satisfied with Tongo as a witness. It was to prove an agonising wait.

What were we to do? I pondered night after night about how Nilam, Ami, Anish and all the other Hindochas who loved Anni so much, would be able to live their lives without the full story of how she had died.

The key figure in all this was Shrien. If he left Cape Town in this way we would never know the full truth about Anni's murder. I was never going to speak to him again. He was a disgusting individual for the way he cheated us and Anni. This was my last chance of getting him to speak to the court.

I had asked the media not to approach me during the trial on the night before it began. But I needed to let the judge know my feelings and that she should not torture me forever by ending the case halfway through. I talked to Ashok, who was already back in Sweden because of the pressures from his hotel business. We agreed we had to speak out.

Ashok would engage with his media contacts from Sweden. Anish, together with his three cousin brothers, would talk to the press in Cape Town.

With our four years of dealing with the media we knew the power and range it enjoyed and hoped these words would pressure the judge into carrying on with the trial.

Anni had to be on the front pages in the days before the judge made her decision. It had all been about Shrien. It was time to remember the real victim of this whole hideous episode.

Anish and his cousin brothers went to a hotel conference room to meet the press and it was broadcast live on television. I saw what he had to say on the TV back at the flat with Nilam. They looked so smart and handsome in their suits with Anni's photograph pinned to their jackets.

Once again I was so proud of Anish. He had shared every bit of pain that his mother and Ami and I had. He was doing what he felt was expected of him and that was demanding justice for his sister. He did not want to look back in the years to come and think he had not used every opportunity to make the judge listen.

Anish spent the few days after the adjournment pacing up and down, wondering what he could do to help.

He was anxious about talking to reporters and their cameras but he was determined and said he knew these days would be our last chance to compel Shrien to talk. He asked Nilam and me to try to relax and let him do his bit in his own way. His prepared statement was powerful and delivered with the right amount of anger, hope and love for Anni.

He said: "I, as Anni's brother, fully expect the South African trial against Shrien Dewani to continue and for his application to end the case to be dismissed. It would be a terrible development in what has been a four-year wait if we and the people of South Africa are not afforded the full story.

"Shrien Dewani has insisted all along that he would clear his name and his legal team have promised the court since the trial began dozens of times that he would help the court with his own version of events.

"The phrase 'my client will tell the court' has become like a mantra to the judge, media and members of the public who have attended the Western Cape Court.

"Well, let's have him 'tell the court' then. That has been his pledge throughout. It would be wrong for him to walk away from South Africa without explaining himself what happened on the night of Anni's murder in this country.

"The people here have been fantastic in their support of us as Anni's family. We cannot thank them enough for the warmth they have shown us and we really appreciate it. Thousands of messages arrive through social media and other means and they mean a lot. Every single one of them.

"But they also show that South Africa, after spending a vast amount of money, time and expertise on bringing Shrien Dewani to trial, is demanding the full story. If they are not given the full facts and by that I mean Shrien Dewani telling the court his version, then Anni's death will remain on the conscience of South Africa forever.

"It will also mean a lifetime of further torture for me and my family, particularly my parents. There have been reports that we as a family are planning to take legal action of our own and sue Shrien Dewani after this murder trial is over. This is not the right time to discuss this and it something we may consider in the future. However, our motivation is not, and never has been, financial. We just demand the truth. And we do that with heavy hearts after such a long time.

"There has been a petition against the judge in this case and we would like to point out it has nothing to do with our own quest for justice and the full story and we have no comment or criticism to make on that or the judge.

"Please allow us the opportunity to demand justice for my sister. Please allow us the full story.

"We have been promised it for four painful years which have devastated our lives. I worry about my parents' health and they need this closure.

"My message is simple. Don't let Shrien Dewani walk away without giving us, South Africa and people all over the world the full story. Let the law take its course."

His plea was strong, passionate and spoken from the heart. But in my own heart I knew it would fall on deaf ears.

Chapter 31

The verdict is in

Cape Town, South Africa
November, 2014

The two-week break and lengthy court adjournments allowed us time to regain our strength and reflect. Nilam and I, along with Anish, Sneha, her husband and some doctor friends from Sweden, made a secret weekend trip to the Kruger safari park where Anni had stayed before flying to Cape Town.

It helped us to see where she had eaten and relaxed and view the sights she had taken in. We wanted to go back to a place where she had been happy. We were warmly greeted by the staff there who knew all about our tragedy and told us how lovely Anni had been while staying there.

It did us all no end of good to escape Cape Town. The privacy helped take our minds off the trial for a few days. The last few days before the decision were fraught and we were very tense. But I stuck to my routine of making eggs at breakfast for the family and catching up on emails on my iPad. The name Dewani was always on our Google searches as we looked for any hope of the judge making the right decision.

Throughout the previous fortnight, after the judge had

adjourned saying that Tongo was an unsatisfactory chief prosecution witness, I had been preparing myself for a devastating ending to our four-year quest for justice.

But I could never have predicted such a savage and wounding finale to the case against Shrien and the dashing of our hopes for the truth.

On December 8, 2014, we were going to find out whether the defence 174 application was going to be discharged or not.

Nilam, Anish and I were driven to the court by police in the same vehicle that had been used to transport my son-in-law to his prison hospital exactly eight months earlier. We were accompanied by Ami, who had left her husband and children in Stockholm to return to Cape Town for the verdict. We hardly spoke at all during the journey because we were too nervous about the judge's impending decision.

Ashok's son Nikesh and my sister's son Amit, who lives with his family in Ilford, were also with us for support.

We expected there would be more significant interest on that day than on any other, but as we pulled up outside the Western Cape Court and climbed the ten steps into the building, the street was swamped with television cameras, journalists, photographers, anti-violence campaigners and the public.

I caught a quick glimpse of people holding photographs of Anni in heart-shaped frames. That was so kind and thoughtful of them.

We were aware the pictures of us arriving were being transmitted around the world but I was determined only to go straight into the building and get this formality over with as quickly as possible. It was going to be very difficult but we had to be there for Anni. There was no question of us missing it.

The police had to form a line to escort us through the entrance. As we struggled to manoeuvre our way through, I thought: "This is all about my innocent daughter Anni. What an impression she has made on the world."

It had been a fortnight since the last time we were in court. That period of waiting had been so extremely brutal to us. We suspected in our heart of hearts that, with the judge's dim view of the prosecution, the case was 95 percent over. But we had still taken the step of speaking out about why the case had to continue – to give us the full story and finally some closure. We desperately hoped the judge would hear us and realise how important our wishes were. We still hoped deep inside that we were wrong. That the judge would let the case continue.

But now it was time for us to remain silent and listen to the judge deliver her verdict. No matter how much we had steeled ourselves, nothing could have prepared us for the decision when it came.

We took our place on the bench to the right of the judge and I saw the Dewani family on the other side. Every seat was taken in the three media boxes and the public gallery above us.

The court had allowed a television camera to broadcast the judge giving her decision on whether to grant the 174 application to Shrien or to reject it, along with all her reasons. The camera was to have its lens fixed on her only.

When Shrien entered, I was glad that the judge made him stand for part of the hearing as she revealed her decision. Because of the elevated position of the dock, and because he was mostly sitting during the trial, we had been able to see his face for the past two months only when he entered or left the courtroom.

Now I could see him. And he could see me. I stared long and hard at him, the judge's droning voice fading into the background, and thought this is the man they say murdered my daughter. This is the man who left his wife in her hour of need. This man cheated on her with gay prostitutes. This man surfed gay websites on his laptop on his honeymoon and a few hours after his wife had been shot dead. This man didn't allow me and my wife to say a proper goodbye to Anni on our own. This man threw out letters from the coffin during the funeral. This man didn't let my daughter Ami speak at the memorial. This man threw a pizza party celebrating Anni's life instead of mourning her death. This man treated Anni with total disrespect. This man went to the shopping mall to buy a new suit instead of accompanying me to the morgue to see Anni's body. This man is a terrible person. Why did he come into our lives?

The judge was in no rush to deliver her decision and sometimes our hopes would be lifted as she went through the evidence. I could see the reporters to our left were also puzzled as to which way it would go. It seemed the only people who really knew were the judge and her two assistants.

But I knew. I had prepared myself for Shrien being freed to return to his home in Westbury-on-Trym. I consoled myself with the thought that at least no other father will ever be taken in by this individual.

It took two hours for her to deliver the words we had dreaded. She barely looked up at the court as she read and stumbled over her words, first saying that Monde Mbolombo had been granted immunity against prosecution, but then correcting herself by adding that he would not be immune from prosecution.

I didn't really care about this lying person, at this point in time, who had put together the hitmen who took Anni's life and then sat back while the others were sent to jail after he'd helped the police. He might be going to jail too and that was something I would have to deal with at a later stage.

But the judge was almost bitter in her criticism of the prosecution as she came towards the end of her two hour address, which had been interrupted only by the customary tea break.

I knew the world was watching when she said she realised there had been strong public opinion that Shrien should be placed into the witness box. This would surely have put her under extraordinary pressure to continue.

At least my public campaign over the previous fortnight to make him take the oath had been noted by her.

But she said that would not be fair on him, or legally correct. "I've heard the plight of the Hindochas," she told the court. But she had also taken an oath and had to apply the law.

Really? Well then listen to us. Make him tell us the truth. Don't let him out of South Africa. You are not satisfied at having to release him. So don't do this to us.

If only she could have read my mind. She would have known the torment erupting inside of me and my family, who were close to tears. She went on to say that the trio who took Anni's life may have been amateurs but she didn't accept they would carry out a murder for just a few thousand rand.

They were bright men and this intelligence made them more than capable of twisting the truth. But that was exactly the point that she missed. These were uneducated people who were in desperate need of money. How can you make a judgement by only hearing one side of the story?

Shrien was about to walk free with so many questions remaining. I was dazed and the room was beginning to spin as once again tears followed their regular route down my face.

Shrien Dewani was about to be released. His lucky number was 174. The judge was saying the evidence against him was "riddled with contradictions."

I just wanted her to deliver the answer and to just get on with it so we could escape before we drowned in our own tears.

She said she regretted that so many details remained unclear surrounding Anni's murder. That gave me no comfort at all, it only made me more puzzled. I believed it was the court's job to clear up any of those uncertainties and this had not been achieved. The questions might have been answered if she had allowed the case to reach a natural conclusion with prosecution, defence and then a verdict.

We were being failed by her, the prosecution, the police, by everybody and everything. And now the rest of our lives were to be decided in the next few sentences.

The words did not come soon enough but they still struck so painfully. Announcing her ruling, the judge said: "There is no evidence on which a court acting reasonably could convict.

"There have been so many mistakes, lies and inconsistencies that one simply cannot know where the lies end and the truth begins."

Then, after only hearing half a court case, she gave her final, definitive decision: "The accused is found not guilty of this charge."

If I had not been sitting down, my legs would have buckled and I would have fallen to the floor. I looked at my family and saw their pain. Everybody was beginning to move around me. But everything was silent in my head. I saw Dewani walk towards the exit of the dock and disappear down the stairs, refusing to look at us as he passed.

They let him slip out of the Western Cape Court without telling us what happened. He had no need to offer a defence and that was an appalling failure by the South Africans.

Ami, Anish and Nilam were in tears and I saw Dewani's defence barrister Van Zyl shaking hands with prosecutor Mopp. The judge disappeared to her left and through her door and then it was all over. It seemed as if it was all happening in slow motion but it was over in just seconds.

That was justice administered the South African way. Everybody would move on except for my family. Tomorrow some other accused would sit in that dock and perhaps another distraught family would take our place. It was indeed a godforsaken and miserable place.

But we had been left to come to terms with the fact that the rest of our lives would be filled with doubt and a feeling of being cheated, never knowing the full story of what happened to Anni.

Three men had been found guilty of murdering her and the fourth, whom they all implicated, had just walked to his freedom. How did this happen?

We had never accused Shrien of killing her. But we did

accuse him of failing her and cheating her. I thought it would have been in his own selfish interest to take the witness box and try to clear up any misconception about his behaviour, rather than live the rest of his life under a question mark.

We were taken to an ante room, where we could not stop crying. I was told that Preyen and Preyal had hugged as we left, in celebration of their brother's release.

I decided we had to go out of the front door and with our heads held high in spite of the series of blows we had suffered as a family in the last four years.

Ami produced a piece of paper on which she had scribbled some thoughts and said she would talk to the media outside. The rest of us were grateful that she could take the lead as we were in shock and it was difficult to think straight, let alone address the world.

But that is exactly what my brave eldest daughter did. She walked in front of us and on the fifth step outside the court talked with dignity and resolve.

People around us shouted "Justice for Anni' and "murderer" outside the court building as the media gathered. Nilam was stuck in the melee with my nephews at the back and with Anish at her side. At that moment Ami restored my family's pride with one of the most passionate and honest of speeches.

Live on news channels across the world, Ami somehow found the strength to say: "Today we feel as a family that the justice system has failed us and we are deeply disappointed. We came here looking for answers and we came here looking for the truth and all we got was more questions.

"We waited patiently for four years to hear what really happened to Anni and to hear the full story of what happened to our dearest little sister.

"All we wanted was to hear all the events. The hope of actually finding that out has kept us, as a family, going. Unfortunately we believe that this right has now been taken away from us because we never heard the full story of Shrien. We heard that Shrien has led a double life and that Anni knew nothing about it.

"And we just wish that Shrien had been honest with us and especially with Anni. Not ever knowing what happened to my dearest little sister on the 13th of November, 2010 – that's going to haunt me, my family, my brother, my parents, for the rest of our lives.

"We've had four years of sleepless nights and... will we ever be able to sleep?"

She stated clearly that we had not demanded that Shrien be found guilty as it mattered little to us and we accepted that he had been cleared. But he should have given us the truth.

Ami had perfectly summed up every feeling I had in my heart at that very moment and I leaned on Anish's back and wept like a baby. I had a mixture of pride at the way Ami and Anish had just faced the world and tears for the lonely existence we would face from now on without our Anni, and without justice.

Captain Louise Smith, who had looked after us by being by our side throughout, hurried us back into the van. As we waited for the driver to take us away, Alex Crawford, the Sky News South Africa correspondent who was broadcasting live, threw the question at me of whether we felt let down.

I shouted: "Yes, yes, yes" as Anish reached to slide the door firmly shut. It was to be my only public comment of the day and I hoped it hadn't come across as rude.

All the way back to the apartment we cried and cried. There was no room for words.

Ashok issued a stern statement to the media from Mariestad. I felt it summed up the turn of events perfectly and paid tribute to Anni. It was designed to keep Anni at the forefront of this terrible day and to nullify any potential celebrations from the Dewani family.

He said: "Anni was a very, very special daughter, sister, niece, cousin, aunty and friend to all who knew and loved her. She easily gave love back and will always be best remembered for her beautiful smile that could light up a room instantly.

"It was a terrible and early end to her young life when she was shot dead in Gugulethu in November 2010 while riding in the back of a taxi on her honeymoon.

"Since that extremely painful day, her family and friends have endured a long wait and sleepless nights over more than four years to learn the full story of how she met her death and for justice to be delivered.

"With the ending of the case against Shrien Dewani today, her family who are in Cape Town will return home with sleepless nights for the rest of their lives. More questions than answers is what we got from this court.

"We do not feel we have been presented with the whole story. The decision to end the trial without the defendant offering a defence means we, and the good people of South Africa, the UK and various parts of the world who have followed the case, will always live without ever knowing the complete events that led up to Anni's death.

"After Shrien Dewani was accused of murder, we would

have preferred him to go into the witness box and tell in his words what happened.

"We know now that he was having gay sex with male prostitutes and declared himself bisexual on the first day of his trial. We would have preferred to have known about his sexuality before he married our precious Anni. She gave herself to him, mind, body and soul and she hoped to have been cherished and loved.

"But she would not have married him if she had known about his secret sex life with male prostitutes and the activities he engaged in. Neither would we, as a family, have condoned a union with a man who indulged himself in such a sordid manner.

"We will now go through this case with our lawyers to confirm whether we can file a lawsuit against Shrien Dewani in the UK.

"As far as Anni's grief-stricken parents are concerned, they would not wish the torture they have endured on any other mother of father. They will live forever with the warm and magical memories of Anni but these memories will always be tinged with the pain of the fact that closure has not been afforded them."

Ashok ended by requesting the media to please refrain from contacting his family in Cape Town, to allow us some respite and space after the traumatic events of this day.

Inside the apartment we all just sat down on the sofa. None of us were hungry or felt like doing anything. We were all speechless. Our heads were spinning around and we did not really know what to do next. I went out on our balcony and looked at the mountain. Not even that beautiful scenery could comfort me now. I had no words, I was totally empty inside.

There was no escape. If we turned away we would be left with our own sadness. If we watched the television we were confronted with it again, although the analysis and interpretation was comforting because it was apparent the judge's decision was not a popular one and there was scant support for Shrien in South Africa.

Nilam and I were wrecked both emotionally and physically and could do nothing but sit down and reflect on where we were and how we had got there.

I stared at Anni's huge photograph beside the giant television set and prayed for her silently.

My sister telephoned from her newsagent's shop in London's Hackney and her voice and words were incredibly soothing, particularly when she reminded me that God would look after Anni and ensure she was happy and at peace.

I adore and love my sister and we would regularly chat for hours on the telephone as I often sought her counsel on family matters. It was wonderful to hear her voice.

Ashok, diligent and assiduous to the end, was on the telephone, repeatedly inquiring if any of us could help him with the massive number of media requests he was receiving. With the exception of a few individuals, the press overall had been very helpful, sensitive and informative. Ashok was right when he said we needed to meet them halfway, despite the terrible situation we were in.

It was agreed that Ami and Anish would meet the press. That evening, only a few hours after the disaster in the courtroom, they went through countless interviews to ensure Anni was the talk of the world.

They did several TV and radio interviews, with all the major news channels, I could not keep track of it all.

Ami and Anish briefed them on how they felt let down by the south African justice system, Shrien's behaviour and how he had denied us the dignified funeral for Anni we would have wished for as well as ultimately denying us the truth and any real closure.

It would have been extremely difficult for them both. But I knew they were doing it for Anni, the sister they adored. They had been through a horrible ordeal and the sight of them both crying on the steps outside the court will live me with always.

Ami left soon afterwards and Anish a few days later. Nilam and I were the last to leave South Africa for what was surely the final time.

On the way to the airport I looked outside the window and whispered to myself: "Goodbye, Anni." I wanted to go to Gugulethu to say goodbye to her one more time but I decided to leave it. I was too exhausted and emotional. Somehow I felt that I was leaving Anni behind and I didn't want to do that. But in reality I know she is in heaven. I do hope her soul finds some peace after all the betrayals.

On the long plane trip back I just felt empty. I feared what would happen when I arrived home. It is a home where I feel safe and where I can try to move on, but also a home where I had lived in hope for the last four years.

I somehow have to teach myself to live with this pain inside, and with the strength and support from my family, I will probably manage to do it.

But I don't know how to move on. All my friends and

colleagues asked about this trip and what happened. I have had to stand up and explain to all of them something which is not easy to explain. I have had to go through it so many times and many have tried to offer advice. There is no simple account to give. It was a mess and a brutal, merciless game played out with our hearts and our lives.

Justice was not delivered. We did not get the answers we were promised as the suspect walked away and was allowed to close the door on us.

However, there were three pluses. My wife made me proud with her strength through it all. Also Ami and Anish had been pillars of support. They always will be. Their sister would have been proud of them too.

Chapter 32

Looking back, and looking forward

Christmas 2014
Mariestad, Sweden

The year of 2015 is almost upon us and despite all that has gone before there is much to look forward to. But there will always be pain and the sense of injustice.

I have been blessed with the sound of the laughter of my grandchildren for the last few days as they and their parents have been visiting for the winter holiday period.

There is heavy snow outside and the temperature is minus 12C. The grandchildren are safe here under my gaze. They are warm too and the sight of them playing happily and innocently is vindication that life is worth living. One day I am sure their mother Ami will sit them down and tell them all about their beautiful aunty Anni and how much she loved them. They were very young but they do remember the love Anni showered them with. They will never forget her.

The long journey home has finally come to an end for us too. The first thing I did on returning to Mariestad was to go and visit my own mother, Ba. She comforted me in the way only a mother can and it was very emotional. We talked through what

happened in South Arica and she reminded me, as always:
"There is a God. Have faith."

I finally reached our home. I opened the door and entered.
My wife and I looked at each other. It felt strange to be here
after such a long time. I walked into the living room and there
on the table was Anni's shrine. Nilam lit a candle for her, just
as she has done each day for the last four years. Anni looks so
beautiful in the picture, wearing a white dress.

I had been given some photos and hand-painted pictures of
Anni from different people who I met in Cape Town. I walked
straight to her room and placed the pictures there, where
everything remains just the same as it was the day she died.
But we are four years on now. Something has to change. We
cannot go on like we have, longing, hoping and praying for
justice.

I hope my family's pain will subside and become
manageable. Right now we smile through the hurt, unclear
if the loss of Anni will always devastate us to the same, huge
extent that it does right now.

That loss has been compounded by gross injustice. Why
was the case dismissed in South Africa? My daughter was
murdered there and nobody can tell me definitively why. It's
just not fair. We will always feel that.

A lot of people die every day and the many left behind do
not always know what happened to their loved ones.

Somehow it's really hard to digest the fact that we went all
the way to South Africa on the promise we would hear what
happened to Anni and we left feeling empty and without any
answers.

I feel so let down, for me, Nilam, Ami and Anish, all the

other Hindochas and the millions around the world who shared our grief.

People will see me smiling but that will be on the outside. There is a big hole in my heart and I don't know how to fill it with anything. I feel as if my body and my soul are shattered too. Empty. Nothing and nobody will ever be able to fill that space. I am in a vacuous shell.

I am almost entirely numb and only my grandchildren tickling me, laughing and giggling, can make me forget for a moment or two. They will return to Stockholm and Nilam and I will look for a way to fill the void again. I will keep on looking and searching.

I left South Africa feeling bitter and that feeling persists. Nobody from the South African prosecution even once stopped to say to me these words: "Mr Hindocha, I am so sorry that we couldn't get justice for your daughter, though we tried our best."

My disappointment at the way the whole case was handled is huge. I just feel so let down. They provided me with excuses of why the trial didn't go so well. They had to rely on criminals to win their case but they had known that for four years. There was enough time to prepare. And four years is ample time to ensure the court microphones are working on day one.

It was a shambolic start to a case that was being followed around the world and it put South African justice in a very poor light from beginning to end. All I ever asked for was the truth and the whole facts. I never got them.

Now I look at Nilam over there playing with our grandchildren. Her smile cannot mask her sadness. Ami's eyes are constantly swollen by the tears that she holds in. Anish is quieter these days, always deep in thought. My son is consumed with anger and I feel helpless because I do not know how to help him.

It's heartbreaking. I always feel proud of my daughter and son. Ami and Anish are so dignified and so strong. But they too didn't get what they sought and what they were promised.

I had hoped the trial in South Africa would have put an end to our misery, allowed us some sleep and the strength to live again.

Instead I have not slept peacefully one single night since returning and I am, right now, just a broken man. I don't know how to get back up on my legs again and all I feel is sadness. I know I still have two wonderful children who I care so much about, but Anni, my middle child, was a part of my heart, part of me.

I have had hope for the last four years that I would find the truth of what happened to her. All that hope is now gone. My daughter, betrayed by someone she loved, left in a car, alone and betrayed by the man who was supposed to love her.

Her death should remain on the conscience of the country where she was murdered. It is a country which failed me and did not produce justice for her.

Looking out of the window at the streets where she used to play as a child, I again whisper to myself: "You are always in my heart, my mind, my thoughts and I will always keep you close. I will not fail you again, Anni. You deserve justice.

"My heart is heavy. I failed you Anni. I am so sorry but I failed you. I didn't get you the justice that you deserve. I did my best but it wasn't enough."

She looks so happy in all the pictures around me. Her smile makes my heart melt. She was so selfless. My sadness turns into anger again. What a coward he was. No matter what happens I will never forgive Shrien for not protecting my daughter and for not telling her the truth about his sexuality.

Such a coward, so afraid of coming out. Their marriage and honeymoon in South Africa is the reason Anni died. A selfish reason and a fate which she didn't deserve. He was a cheat who took the hand of my daughter. She should have been adored. Instead she was left in the hands of murderers who placed no value on life.

If he had been honest with her she would have walked away and never met her death in South Africa. Thank God, Anni, you were never formally married so you remained a Hindocha. One of us. Not one of his.

I close my eyes and take another deep breath. Oh, Anni, I miss you so much, my beloved angel. I know you are looking down on us. One day I believe you will come back to us, one way or another. All I can do until then is to remember you for the bubbly, smiling, exciting, creative, passionate, selfless and honest person you were.

Your personality always made me smile and you were so full of life. You had the biggest heart I have ever seen in a human being, always thinking of everyone else before yourself.

You had style and always dressed like a model. You loved your family and always put the family first, and the family loved you back just as much.

You were so kind, so sweetly naive and so honest and these are the qualities and memories of you that I will keep close to my heart always.

I love you. I always have and I always will. You have left a big hole in my heart and that will stay for as long as I live.

One day we will be together again. Rest in peace. My beloved daughter Anni.

ABOUT THE AUTHOR

SHEKHAR BHATIA is a London born journalist who has been on the staff of the Evening Standard, Sunday Mirror, Daily Express, the Observer and the Sunday Express where he was Chief Reporter.

He began his journalistic career at the age of 17 on the Waltham Forest Guardian in East London and worked in the old Fleet Street from the age of 22.

Shekhar has produced documentaries for British and American TV companies on subjects such as the Oscar Pistorius shooting of Reeva Steenkamp for NBC and the BBC. He also helped produce Channel Four's Dispatches TV programme on Anni's death, entitled "Murder on Honeymoon."

Shekhar has spent four years on the murder story, working closely with Anni's family, who asked him to help them write this book.

He describes himself as the "luckiest reporter in the world" for having had the opportunity to travel the globe meeting his heroes, including the late Nelson Mandela in his Presidential mansion while flying around Southern Africa on a private jet with the Prince of Wales.

Shekhar has also reported from five World Cups including the most recent in Brazil and five Olympics. In November 2014, he was named Journalist of the Year at the Asian Media Awards. He is a lifelong supporter of West Ham United, lives in London with his student daughter Chameli and is set to move to New York later in 2015 for work.